THE
POWER
TO
CHANGE
YOUR
LIFE

THE
POWER
TO
CHANGE
YOUR
LIFE

RICK WARREN

While this book is intended for the reader's personal enjoyment and profit, it is also intended for group study. A leader's guide with Reproducible Response Sheets is available from your local bookstore or from the publisher.

VICTOR BOOKS®
A DIVISION OF SCRIPTURE PRESS PUBLICATIONS INC.
USA CANADA ENGLAND

Unless otherwise noted, Scripture quotations are from the *Holy Bible, New International Version,* © 1973, 1978, 1984, International Bible Society. Used by permission of Zondervan Bible Publishers. Other quotations are from the *Authorized (King James) Version* (KJV); the *Good News Bible* (GNB)—Old Testament: © American Bible Society 1976; New Testament: © American Bible Society 1966, 1971, 1976; The *New King James Version* (NKJV), © 1979, 1980, 1982, Thomas Nelson, Inc., Publishers; the *Revised Standard Version of the Bible* (RSV), © 1946, 1952, 1971, 1973; *The Living Bible* (TLB), © 1971, Tyndale House Publishers, Wheaton, IL 60189, used by permission; *The New Testament in Modern English* (PH), Revised Edition, © J.B. Phillips, 1958, 1960, 1972, permission of Macmillan Publishing Co. and Collins Publishers; and *The Bible: A New Translation* © 1922, 1924, 1925, 1926, 1935 by Harper & Row, Publishers, Inc. © 1950, 1952, 1953, 1954 by James A.R. Moffatt (MOFFATT).

Library of Congress Cataloging-in-Publication Data

Warren, Richard, 1954-
  The power to change your life / by Rick Warren.
    p.   cm.
  ISBN 0-89693-472-1
  1. Christian life—1960- 2. Fruit of the Spirit. I. Title.
BV4501.2.W3762   1990
248.4—dc20   90-32493
                                                          CIP

1 2 3 4 5 6 7 8 9 10 Printing/Year 94 93 92 91 90

Contents

Dedication

To Amy, Joshua, and Matthew.
I am so proud of each of you.
My prayer is that your lives will
demonstrate the message of this book.

Chapter One

THE POWER
TO CHANGE YOUR LIFE!

What would you like to change about yourself? Would you like to be more confident, more relaxed? Perhaps you'd like to be more outgoing, less anxious, or less fearful. Most of us are more than a little interested in changing because we realize there is always room for improvement.

Why Can't I Change?

In the years I have been a pastor, the number one question I'm asked is, "Rick, why can't I change? I want to change, I really do. But I don't know how—or I don't have the power."

We go to seminars and conferences, looking for the painless cure that is going to zap our lives and change us by instantly giving us self-discipline. Or we go on diets. I once went on a diet for an entire afternoon.

We join health clubs and our enthusiasm runs strong for about two weeks. Then we fall back into the same old rut. We don't change. We read self-help books, but the problem with self-help books is that they tell us *what* to do but they can't give us the *power* to do it. They say things like: "Get rid of all your bad habits, be positive, don't be negative." But how? Where do I get the power to change? How do I get my life out of neutral? How do I break out of the mold that I'm in? Good news. Christianity offers the power we need.

You Can Have Resurrection Power

The word *power* occurs 57 times in the New Testament. It is a word used to describe the most powerful event that ever happened. An event that separated A.D. from B.C. That event was the resurrection of Jesus Christ from the dead. And that resurrection power is available to change your life!

The most important thing in life is knowing Christ and experiencing the power of His resurrection. Paul writes, "I want to know Christ and the *power* of His resurrection" (Phil. 3:10). In another letter Paul writes, "I pray that you will begin to understand how incredibly great His power is to help those who believe Him. It is the same mighty power that raised Christ from the dead and seated Him in the place of honor at God's right hand in heaven" (Eph. 1:19-20, TLB).

Paul uses the Greek word for power, *dunamis,* which is the root of our word *dynamite.* So Paul is saying, "God wants to give you dynamite power in your life, the power that can change your life." Yes, the same power that raised Jesus Christ from the dead 2,000 years ago is available to you right now to transform the weaknesses in your life into strengths. The Bible describes resurrection power as the power to cancel your past, the power to conquer your problems, and the power to change your personality.

God's Power Will Cancel Your Past

First, resurrection power is the power to cancel your past. I'm talking about your failures, your mistakes, your sins, your regrets. And when I say *cancel,* I'm not talking about denying the past as if it never happened. The word *cancel* means to eliminate, to neutralize, to offset something.

Have you ever gotten halfway through a project and wished you could start over? You're painting the living room, and you step back and look at the color that looked perfect on the sample chart. On the wall, however, it doesn't look so perfect. You wish you could just start over.

A lot of people feel that way about life: "I've made so many mistakes. I wish I could just wipe them out and start over."

The failures, the problems, the bad decisions—we've all suffered from them.

Some people just can't seem to let go of their past and, as a result, they let their past limit their present opportunities. They live in a constant state of regret. They continually say, "If only I hadn't done that" or "If only I had made these changes." They always second-guess themselves. They are tormented by painful memories: "I blew it, and I'm going to be paying for it the rest of my life."

God says it's unnecessary for us to go around with a heavy load of guilt, and old hurts, or memories of mistakes. In Colossians 2:14 He says He has forgiven all our sins and canceled every record of the debt we had to pay. He did it by allowing Christ to be nailed to the cross.

Jesus Christ knows the things you've done wrong, but He did not come to rub them in. He came to rub them out. He did not come to condemn you; He came to change you. A clean slate is possible! It's a lot like my son's Etch A Sketch. If he makes a mess of a design or picture, all he has to do is flip it over to wipe the slate clean. Then he can start all over again. The Bible says that is what God does with the mistakes I've made. When I come to Him, He wipes the slate clean.

In Jeremiah 31:34 God says to the Israelites that He "will remember their sins no more." That's got to be one of the most amazing statements in the Bible—that the God who made the world "forgets." Today when we come to Him, admit our sins to Him, and then ask Him to forgive us, He cancels our past. God *chooses* to forget our wrongs, our mistakes, our failures. That's good news! Even if you were to die tonight and stand before God in heaven, you could ask Him about some sin you committed yesterday, and He would say, "What sin?"

He has canceled your past and set you free to get on with the present.

Why God Can Cancel Your Past

Now what is the basis of this forgiveness?

When Jesus died, one of His last statements from the cross was, "It is finished" (John 19:30). In the Greek that's one word, *tetelestai,* literally meaning "paid in full," "canceled." It was the word merchants wrote on bills when they were paid: "paid in full." It was stamped on a document concerning a prison sentence that had been commuted. Jesus says that's what He did on the cross: He paid in full for every sin you've ever made. Romans 8:1 tells us: "Therefore, there is now no condemnation for those who are in Christ Jesus." Jesus was crucified on the cross so you can stop crucifying yourself. He was hung for your hang-ups. That's good news!

Now the question is: If God forgets a sin the moment you confess it, don't you think you ought to forget it too? How long do you remember a bill you have paid? I forget my bills as soon as they've been paid. I don't worry about last month's electric bill. Someone has said that when we give God all our mistakes and failures, He throws them into the deepest part of the sea. Then He puts up a sign that says *No Fishing.* He doesn't want us to keep dredging up our sins.

Paul said, "Forgetting what is behind . . . I press on toward the goal to win the prize for which God has called me heavenward in Christ Jesus" (Phil. 3:13-14). We can short-circuit God's power in our lives by not believing God has truly forgiven us or by choosing not to forgive ourselves. God's power is the power to cancel your past.

God's Power Will Conquer Your Problems

God's power is also the power to conquer your problems. Everyone has problems. They come with living in a fallen world. If you don't think you have any problems, check your pulse. (The only people who don't have problems are in cemeteries)

Our real problem is what we do with our problems. Inevitably, we try to solve them with our own power. How do you know when you're trying to solve all your problems with your own strength? You're tired all the time! A man who was frustrated with his lack of power to conquer his problems summed it up when he said, "I'm sick and tired of being sick and tired." We get this way when we try to solve our problems on our own. God wants us to stop _trying_ and start _trusting_ Him with our problems.

I have met thousands of people who feel like their lives are out of control. They tell me, "My life is out of control; I'm a victim of my circumstances. What can I do? I'm powerless. Just about the time I make ends meet, somebody moves the ends." If you ask them, "How are you doing?" they respond, "I'm doing okay, _under_ the circumstances." Well, what are they doing _under_ them? Someone has said circumstances are like a mattress: if you're on top, you rest easy, but if you get underneath, you suffocate! A lot of people are _under_ their circumstances. Although we cannot always control our circumstances, we can control how we respond to them.

You might be saying, "But, Rick, you don't know all the problems I'm going through. I'm having a really tough time." If so, let me encourage you to take the focus off your problems and focus on God's promises.

Look at what Paul asks in Romans 8:35: "Who shall separate us from the love of Christ? Shall trouble or hardship or persecution or famine or nakedness or danger or sword?" He answers his question in verse 37: "No, in all these things we are more than conquerors through Him who loved us." Do you know what the word _conquer_ means? A conqueror is "one who overcomes by gaining control." Paul says that we are _more than_ conquerors. The Greek word explains that we are _super_ conquerors and that we can have _overwhelming_ victory. If we put our lives in God's hands and rely on the power of the

Resurrection, nothing can devastate us. *Nothing* can swallow us up or destroy us. That's the message of the Resurrection and the heart of the Good News.

No matter how dark the situation may be, God can turn it around. No matter how hopeless life *seems*, God brings hope. The same power that enabled Jesus Christ to rise from the dead will allow you to rise above your problems.

Acts 4 records the first serious opposition to the apostles' preaching of the Gospel in Jerusalem. When the authorities threatened them, they banded together and prayed. But notice what they prayed for. They didn't ask God to stop the opposition but rather to give them supernatural boldness in the face of the opposition (4:29). He did (4:31).

Resurrection power enables you to cancel your past and conquer your problems. But that's not all it does.

God's Power Will Change Your Personality
Resurrection power also helps you change your personality. What would you like to change about yourself, and how do you go about doing it? Let's put it another way: How would your spouse like you to change? Maybe that would be more revealing. One wife said her husband is "too temperamental"—90 percent temper and 10 percent mental! In another situation, a husband went in for marriage counseling one day and told his pastor he wanted a divorce. The pastor reminded him that he had promised before God that he would take his wife for better or for worse. The man said, "Yes, but she's a lot worse than I took her for."

How would you complete this sentence: "It's just like me to . . ."? It's just like me to *be late all the time?* It's just like me to *be unable to stay on a diet?* It's just like me to *put my foot in my mouth?* It's just like me to *blow up,* to *be depressed,* to *get angry?* I'm sure you're well aware of the parts of your personality you'd change if you could.

God Uses a Process

God uses a two-step process to change us. The first step is explained in 2 Corinthians 5:17, "If anyone is in Christ, he is a new creation; the old has gone, the new has come!" When we commit our lives to Christ, that's the initial turning point. We are not the same anymore. A new life has begun. That's why the Bible calls it being "born again." Being born again doesn't mean we are reincarnated; it simply means we get a chance to start over. It's not turning over a new leaf but getting a new life, a fresh start. And it's a new beginning with a big difference: we now have a new nature and the indwelling Holy Spirit. A set of "spiritual batteries" are included to provide the power! That makes all the difference in the world.

Being born again, like being born the first time, is only the beginning. It is followed by a lifetime process described in Romans 12:2. J.B. Phillips paraphrases the verse this way: "Don't let the world around you squeeze you into its own mould, but let God remake you so that your whole attitude of mind is changed. Thus you will prove in practice that the will of God is good, acceptable to Him, and perfect."

In the next chapter we'll examine more specifically how God helps us change and the tools He uses. Then we'll take a close look at how He changes us by producing in us the fruit of the Spirit as listed in Galatians 5:22-23. Each chapter will be devoted to one of these character qualities. When the Holy Spirit controls your life, He will produce in you nine positive characteristics: love, joy, peace, patience, kindness, goodness, faithfulness, gentleness, and self-control.

Let me ask you, how many of the people you work with or live with exhibit these qualities? How many of the people you work with or live with would say these qualities describe you? The sad fact is that rather than loving others, we are often unloving. Rather than living joyously, we feel defeated, depressed, and discouraged. Rather than experiencing peace, we feel uptight and pressured. Rather than being patient, we're frustrated and irritated. Instead of showing kindness, it's every man for himself. Instead of modeling goodness, we often feel there's nothing good about ourselves. Instead of being faithful, we neglect our commitments. We are more likely to respond to others in anger or resentment than in gentleness. And instead of practicing self-control, we watch our lives falling apart.

These are the contrasts between the person who lets the power of God work in his life and the person who relies on his own power. We must remember, however, that the fruit of the Spirit isn't something we work up. It's something that God produces in us when we fully trust Him with our lives.

Don't Put It Off

Only one thing will keep you from changing and becoming the person you and God want you to be. It's not the devil. It's not other people. It's not circumstances. It's procrastination.

I meet so many people who are getting ready to live, but never live. "I'm aiming to change," they tell me. And I want to reply, "That's good, but when are you going to pull the trigger?"

Procrastination is fatal. One of these days I'm going to go to the dentist. One of these days I'm going to have that surgery I need. One of these days I'm going to spend more time with the family . . . get serious about being a Christian . . . become active in church . . . go after that dream. One of these days I'm going to get in shape. One of these days! More often than not, that day never comes.

Why Spend One More Night with the Frogs?

One of my favorite movies is *The Ten Commandments,* with Charlton Heston standing out there separating the Red Sea so the Israelites can walk through. My family gets a kick out of my behavior every time I see *The Ten Commandments* because for the next couple of weeks I go around walking and talking like Yul Brynner, who portrayed Pharaoh in the movie. When my kids ask me something, I reply, "So let it be written; so let it be done!"

One of the humorous facts about the events surrounding the Israelites' exodus from Egypt concerns the ten plagues God sent on the Egyptians. Each plague made fun of a different Egyptian god. For instance, the Egyptians worshiped lice, so God sent them a lot of lice to worship. Then there was the plague of frogs. The Bible says there were frogs everywhere. It must have been messy! I'm sure Mrs. Pharaoh put pressure on Pharaoh to give in and get rid of the frogs.

Finally, Pharaoh summoned Moses and said, "All right, Moses, I give up." So Moses asked, "When do you want me to get rid of the frogs?" Now Pharaoh's answer was classic. He said, "Tomorrow." He must have been crazy! Why would anyone wait any longer to have the frogs removed?

There's a famous sermon based on this text called "One More Night with the Frogs." How would you like to spend one more night with the frogs? Why in the world would anyone put off a change that was going to be positive? We would have expected Pharaoh to say, "Get rid of the frogs right now!" But no, he said, "Tomorrow."

You and I do this all the time. We procrastinate by putting off changes that we know will be good for us. Why? Maybe we're complacent. Maybe we're too lazy to change. Maybe we're afraid because we don't know what the changes will involve. Maybe we're too proud, or we're just stubborn. Whatever the reason, we procrastinate.

The NASA space engineers tell us that most of the fuel used in a rocket launch is burned up in the first few seconds of lift-off. It takes tremendous energy and thrust to get the rocket off the launchpad. Once it's moving and headed for orbit, it requires much less fuel and is easier to control and direct. It has overcome inertia.

It's one thing for me to tell you that Jesus Christ can cancel your past, help you conquer the problems you are facing right now, and change your personality. But it's quite another matter for you to overcome inertia and actually let Him begin to do it now! Although you may agree with everything I say, you may still wait and let Jesus help you "one of these days."

Jesus Christ has the power to make changes in your life now. He will give you the power to get started and the power to keep going. He will give you the power to break the chains of procrastination.

If you have been unable to let go of your past, Jesus Christ offers complete forgiveness. He can put your life back together again. You may feel like Humpty Dumpty, so fragmented that nothing can put you back together. But it's never too late to start over! You're never a failure until you give up.

Maybe you're overwhelmed by your problems. The Resurrection reminds us that no situation is hopeless. Relax. Trust God. You don't have to be controlled by your circumstances. No problem is too big for God. He's still in the resurrection business. What are you waiting for? Right now you can say: "Jesus Christ, take my life. Take the good, the bad, and the ugly. Take every part of me." Open your heart to His love right now and let His transforming resurrection power become a reality in your life.

Chapter Two

GOD'S PART AND MY PART
IN CHANGING ME

One of my fondest memories of growing up is my father's garden. It seemed my dad grew everything in his garden. In fact, he always grew enough to feed the entire neighborhood. Whenever people would stop by our home for a visit, they'd usually leave with a sack full of fresh vegetables and luscious fruit.

The kind of fruit my father grew is just one kind of fruit— *natural* fruit. There is also *biological* fruit, the offspring of animals and the children of people. Then there is *spiritual* fruit, and that's what God is talking about in Galatians 5:22-23: "But the fruit of the Spirit is love, joy, peace, patience, kindness, goodness, faithfulness, gentleness, and self-control." These nine qualities describe the character of a fruitful, productive Christian.

The question is: how do we get these character qualities? Obviously, God doesn't just zap me one day and all of a sudden these qualities materialize in my life. He uses a process. In this chapter we'll look at that process.

It's a Partnership
The Apostle Paul describes the two-part process God uses in Philippians 2:12-13 where he first says, "Work out your salvation," and then turns around and says, "It is God who works in you." It sounds like a contradiction, doesn't it? But it isn't. It's a paradox. G.K. Chesterton describes a paradox as "truth standing on its head to get attention." Paul loves to teach with paradoxes.

The key to understanding this paradox is the little word *out* in verse 12. Notice that Paul doesn't say, "Work *for* your salvation." That's a big difference. To work *for* something means to earn it, to deserve it, to merit it. The Bible clearly teaches that salvation is not something we have to work for. It is a free gift of God's grace. Paul says, "Work *out* your salvation." Paul is talking about a "spiritual workout."

What do you do in a physical workout? You develop or tone muscles that God has given you. To work out means to cultivate, to make the most of what you have been given. That's what Paul says here. Cultivate your spiritual life!

God has a part in our spiritual growth and we also have a part. He provides the power, but we must flip the switch. Work out your salvation for it is God who works in you.

God Uses His Word

Let's look first at God's part in this process and the tools He uses. Then we'll look at our part and some choices we need to make. The first tool God uses in changing us is the Bible. Through Scripture He teaches us how to live. Second Timothy 3:16-17 tells us, "The whole Bible was given to us by inspiration from God and is useful to teach us what is true and to make us realize what is wrong in our lives; it straightens us out and helps us do what is right. It is God's way of making us well prepared at every point" (TLB).

Has the Bible transformed your life? I heard about a converted cannibal in the South Sea islands who was sitting by a large pot reading his Bible when an anthropologist wearing a pith helmet approached him and asked, "What are you doing?"

The native replied, "I'm reading the Bible."

The anthropologist scoffed and said, "Don't you know that modern, civilized man has rejected that book? It's nothing but a pack of lies. You shouldn't waste your time reading it."

The cannibal looked him over from head to toe and slowly

replied, "Sir, if it weren't for this book, you'd be in that pot!" The Word of God had changed his life, and his appetite.

If you are serious about changing your life, you're going to have to get into the Bible. You need to read it, study it, memorize it, meditate on it, and apply it.

When people tell me their faith is weak, I ask them, "Are you reading your Bible regularly?"

"Not really."

"Are you studying the Bible?"

"Well, not exactly."

"Are you memorizing Scripture?"

"No."

"Well then, how do you expect your faith to grow?" The Bible says, "Faith comes by hearing, and hearing by the Word of God" (Rom. 10:17, NKJV).

God's Part in the Process: His Spirit

The second tool God uses to change us is the Holy Spirit. When we commit ourselves to Christ, the Holy Spirit comes into our lives to empower and direct us (Rom. 8:9-11). The Spirit of God gives us new strength and vitality and the desire and the power to do what is right. As the Spirit of the Lord works within us, we become more and more like Him.

Now if you don't get anything else out of this chapter, get this: God's number one purpose in your life is to make you like Jesus Christ. The Spirit of God uses the Word of God to make the child of God more like the Son of God. And what is Jesus like? His life on earth embodied the ninefold fruit of the spirit: love, joy, peace, patience, kindness, goodness, faithfulness, gentleness, and self-control.

God Uses Circumstances

God's ideal way of changing us is to have us read the Bible to find out how we should live and then depend on His indwelling

Spirit to enable us to do it. Unfortunately, most of us are stubborn, and we don't change that easily. So God brings in a third tool to work on us—circumstances. I'm talking about problems and pressures and heartaches and difficulties and stress. These things always get our attention. C.S. Lewis says that God whispers to us in our pleasure but shouts to us in our pain. It often takes a painful situation to get our attention.

In the Phillips translation, Romans 8:28-29 reads, "To those who love God, who are called according to His plan, everything that happens fits into a pattern for good. For God . . . chose them to bear the family likeness of His Son." Nothing can come into the life of a believer without the Heavenly Father's permission, unless it is "Father-filtered."

The interesting thing about how God uses circumstances is that the source of the circumstances makes no difference to Him. We often bring problems on ourselves by our own faulty decisions and bad judgments and sins. Other times our problems are caused by other people. Sometimes the devil causes things to happen to us as he did to Job. But God says the source of the circumstance is irrelevant. "I will still use it in your life," He says. "I will fit it into My pattern; I will fit it into My great plan for your life, to make you like Jesus Christ." So, there is no circumstance in life from which we can't learn, if we'll just have the right attitude.

Proverbs 20:30 has some more good news: "Blows and wounds cleanse away evil, and beatings purge the inmost being." Perhaps you've experienced the truth of this verse. Sometimes it takes a painful experience to make us change our ways. In other words, we're not as likely to change when we see the light as when we feel the heat! Why? Because we change only when the fear of change is exceeded by our pain.

I wear shoes for comfort, not for style. A few years ago I had a pair of black shoes that I wore almost every day for over a year. I finally started getting holes in the bottom of them, but they were so comfortable I continued to wear them. I wouldn't cross my legs when sitting on a platform so people in the congregation couldn't see the holes. I knew I needed to buy new shoes, but I kept putting it off. Then one week it rained, for the entire week. After four days of soggy socks, I became motivated to change and bought some new shoes. The first step in change is usually discomfort!

God speaks to us through the Bible, and by promptings of His Holy Spirit, but if He can't get our attention, He will also use circumstances. For example, the Bible says that we should be humble, and the Holy Spirit enables us to be humble. But if we don't humble ourselves, He'll use circumstances to humble us. God can use every situation in our lives for our growth. That's His part. Now, what about our part?

We Must Choose Our Thoughts

Spiritual growth is not automatic. Change is a matter of choice. We can't just passively sit around doing nothing and expect to grow. We must make three choices if we really want to change.

First, *we must carefully choose what we think about*. Proverbs 4:23, in the *Good News* translation, says, "Be careful how you think; your life is shaped by your thoughts." Someone once said, "You're not what you think you are, but what you think, you are." Did you get that? You're not what you think you are, but what you think, you are. If you're going to change your life, you have to change your thought patterns. Change always begins with new thinking.

How does a person become a Christian? By repenting. Repentance is often a misunderstood term. I used to think of it as a man standing on a street corner with a sign that says, "Turn or burn!" Actually, the Greek word for repentance is *metanoia*, and it means to change your mind, to change your perspective. When I became a Christian, I changed my perspective on a lot of things. Romans 12:2 states we are transformed by the renewing of our mind. It's not "be transformed by willpower" but "be transformed by the renewing of your mind."

The Bible teaches us that the way you think determines the way you feel, and the way you feel determines the way you act. So if you want to change your actions, you've got to go back to the source and change the way you think. Sometimes you may act depressed. Do you know why? Because you feel depressed. Do you know why you feel depressed? Because you are thinking depressing thoughts. The same is true for anger and worry and all the other kinds of destructive thought patterns.

What I
Think ————————▶
Determines

What I
Feel ————————▶
Determines

How I
Act

Imagine you had a speedboat, and the speedboat had an automatic pilot. The boat is heading east, and you decide you want to go west. You want to make a 180 degree turn. There are two ways to do that. The automatic pilot is heading the boat east, but you could grab the steering wheel and turn it around by sheer force. The boat is now heading west, but the whole time that you're forcing it by willpower to go west, you're under tension. That's because the boat is naturally inclined to go the other way. You're tense and uptight, and soon you get tired. You know what happens then. You let go of the "wheel" and . . . you go off the diet, or you start smoking again, or you stop exercising, or you slip back into your old patterns of relating to your family. The truth is, trying to force yourself to change by sheer willpower seldom produces lasting results.

The other way to change the direction of your boat is to adjust the automatic pilot. Now the "automatic pilot" in your life is your thoughts. How did you finish the sentence I gave you in the first chapter: "It's just like me to be . . ."? You finish that sentence a few times, and I'll tell you what the automatic pilot in your life is set on.

But you can be transformed by the renewing of your mind. Don't focus on your actions. Don't focus on your feelings. People often say, "I'm going to be more loving" or "I'm going to be happy if it kills me." But forcing a feeling doesn't work. Simply focus on changing your thoughts.

When you change your thoughts, you also change the way you feel. I must stop thinking those thoughts that are getting me into trouble and start thinking thoughts that get me where I want to go.

Jesus said, "You will know the truth, and the truth will set you free" (John 8:32). When you base your life on truth—you live with the right kind of thoughts, not misconceptions or false beliefs, and you base your life on right thoughts out of God's Word—you will be set free. You will find your old habits and feelings and actions falling away.

God gives us His Word, but we've got to use it. We've got to practice biblical meditation. When I use the word *meditation,* I'm not talking about sitting in a yoga position and chanting "ummmmmm." You don't need TM or yoga or any of those meditative techniques based on Eastern religions. Stay away from them. Meditate on God's Word. Read through the Book of Psalms and see how many times David says, "I meditate on Your Word day and night."

In Psalm 1 we read: "Blessed is the man who does not walk in the counsel of the wicked or stand in the way of sinners or sit in the seat of mockers." In other words, he doesn't get his input from the wrong sources. "But his delight is in the law of the LORD [the Bible], and on His law he *meditates* day and night" (emphasis added). As a result, "He is like a tree planted by streams of water, which yields its *fruit* in season and whose leaf does not wither. Whatever he does prospers" (emphasis added). That is an amazing promise.

God says that when you meditate on His Word day and night, you will bear fruit. We're talking about being fruitful, productive people—people full of love, joy, peace, patience. . . . He also says you'll prosper. There are two great promises in Scripture about success; one of them is here and the other is in Joshua 1:18. They both say that the key to success is meditating on God's Word.

What then does it mean to meditate on God's Word? If you look up the word *meditation* in a dictionary, you will find that a synonym is the word *rumination*. Rumination is what a cow does when it chews its cud. A cow eats some grass, chews up all that she can, and then swallows it. It sits in one of her stomachs for a while, and then a little bit later she burps it up—with renewed flavor. The cow chews on it some more and swallows it again. That's rumination. That cow is straining every ounce of nourishment out of that grass. That's what meditation is. Meditation is thought digestion. Meditation doesn't mean you put your mind in neutral and think about nothing. Meditation is thinking seriously about what you are reading. You take one verse and ask, "What does this mean for my life?" Talk to yourself about it, and talk to God about it.

God is quite specific in telling us what to think about. In Philippians 4:8 He says we are to think about eight different categories of things and, by implication, to avoid thinking about the opposite kinds of things. Take a few minutes right now to read this verse and think about it. Talk to God about it. This will be good practice in meditating on God's Word.

Colossians 3:16 says, "Let the Word of Christ dwell in you

richly." You need to spend regular time every day, a minimum of 10–15 minutes, where you sit down and read a portion of the Bible and think about what you've just read. Then talk to the Lord about it in prayer. That's the starting point for our part in change. We can choose what we think about.

We Must Depend on His Spirit

We can also *choose to depend on the Holy Spirit.* God says, "I put my Holy Spirit in you to give you power." All Christians have God's Spirit in their lives, but not all Christians have God's *power* in their lives. Jesus gives a beautiful illustration of this in John 15. He compares our spiritual life to a vine and its branches. "I am the vine; you are the branches," He says. "He who abides in Me, and I in him, bears much fruit; for without Me you can do nothing" (John 15:5, NKJV).

In this illustration, the branch is totally dependent on the main vine; it cannot produce fruit by itself. Fruit is an inside job. If I went out in the spring and tied apples on the branches of a dead tree and then took my wife out and said, "Honey, look at our fruit tree," she'd say, "You tied those things on." That's what it's like when a Christian says, "I'm going to tie on a bunch of fruit in my life. A little patience here, a little goodness there, a little self-control here. I'll do it on my own." It can't be done. It's an inside job. Remember, it's the fruit of the Spirit.

Now you might be saying, "How do I know if I am abiding in Christ? How do I know if I'm hooked to the vine? How do I know if I'm depending on His Spirit?" It's simple. Look at your prayer life. Your prayers demonstrate your dependence on God.

What do you pray about? Whatever you pray about is what you're hooked into God about. Whatever you don't pray about is what you're trying to do on your own. Prayer is the acid test.

The secret of depending on God's Spirit is to be incessantly in prayer. Pray about your decisions. Pray about your needs. Pray about your interests. Pray about your schedule. Pray about problems you're facing. Pray about people you're going to meet. Pray about purchases. Pray about everything. That's what it means to abide, to be aware that God is always with us, to practice His presence. As we pray, we will start to see the fruit developing in our lives.

We Must Respond Wisely to Circumstances

In addition to choosing our thoughts and choosing to depend on His Spirit, we can also *choose how we respond to the circumstances of our lives*. Victor Frankl was one of the Jews put in the Nazi concentration camp at Dachau. He says that while he was in the camp, the guards stripped him of everything. They took his identity. They took his wife. They took his family. They took his clothes. They even took his wedding ring. But there was one thing that no one could take from him. He writes, "The last of human freedoms is the ability to chose one's attitude in a given set of circumstances" (*Man's Search for Meaning*, Washington Square Press, p. 12). The guards could not take from Frankl his freedom to choose his attitude.

We cannot control all the circumstances in our lives. We don't know what is going to happen tomorrow, or even today. We cannot control our circumstances, but we can control how we respond to them. We can control whether an experience makes us a bitter person or a better person. What matters in life is not so much what happens *to* us but what happens *in* us.

Paul talks about this in Romans 5:3-4. He says we can rejoice here and now, even in our trials and troubles. These things will produce perseverance in us and help us develop a mature character. So we can rejoice in our problems, not just endure them because we know that God is using them in our lives. God even uses the problems I bring on myself.

God also uses the situation that others mean for bad in my life. That's a lesson from the life of Joseph as told in the Old Testament. Joseph was betrayed by his brothers and sold into slavery. Years later he said, "You intended to harm me, but God intended it for good" (Gen. 50:20). That is also true in your life. Maybe there is somebody right now who is trying to hurt you. Don't worry. If you're a believer, if you have put your life in God's hands, God can even use such a painful situation for good. He will develop within you a mature character. And that's what the fruit of the Spirit is all about. God wants to produce the character of Christ in our lives because He knows the more we become like Him the more fulfilled we will be.

When God created man, He made him "in His own image" (Gen. 1:27). That was God's original plan, and it has not changed. He wants to make us like Himself; not gods, but godly. How does He do it? Through the Bible, through His Holy Spirit, and through circumstances. God works on our character. The Greek word for character in Romans 5:4 means "tested and proven reliable." It describes something that has gone through the fire, something that has been beat on and beat up but stood the test.

Have you seen the luggage commercial on TV which features a gorilla? At the airport a suitcase is shown going out on a conveyor belt, and instead of being picked up gently by a nice gentleman, it is manhandled by a gorilla. He hurls the luggage around the room, stomps on it, jumps on it, and throws it up in the air. Now that luggage has character. It is reliable. It has stood the test. This week you may get beat up at work. You may get knocked around at home, but God can use even these situations in your life.

Let me make a statement here that is one of the most important things I will say to you in the pages of this book. Here is the key truth: God produces the fruit of the Spirit in us by allowing us to encounter situations and people full of exactly the opposite qualities.

How does God produce love in our lives? It's easy to love lovely people or people just like ourselves. But to teach you real love, God will put us around some unlovely people. We will learn real love by loving that cantankerous fellow at work or that pesky neighbor. God will teach us to love by letting us practice on the "unlovely."

The same is true for peace. Anyone can be at peace in peaceful situations. That doesn't take character. God teaches us about peace in the midst of total chaos, when everything is falling apart. The phone rings, the doorbell rings, something is boiling over on the stove, the baby's crying, the dog bit the cat. That's when we can truly learn inner peace. God works the same way for each fruit He is developing in us.

It Takes Time
One last point. It takes time for fruit to ripen. There is no such thing as instant maturity. And there is no such thing as instant spiritual growth. It takes time. When you try to rush fruit, it doesn't taste as good. Have you ever eaten gassed tomatoes? You have, if you've purchased them at the grocery store. If farmers picked ripe tomatoes and shipped them, they would get smashed on the way to market, so they pick them green (maybe I'm revealing a trade secret here) and spray CO_2 gas on them right before they go to market. That gas ripens the green tomato into a red tomato very quickly. Now there is nothing wrong with those tomatoes. But if you've ever eaten a vine-ripened tomato, there is no comparison. It takes time for fruit to ripen. And God is going to need time to ripen the fruit in your life.

You can begin by telling God right now that you want to be a productive, fruitful Christian, that you want to cooperate with His plan. Commit yourself to reading, studying, memorizing, and meditating on the Bible. Ask God to use His Word to change the way you think. Invite the Holy Spirit to have free reign in your life. Don't hold anything back. Pray and talk with Him about everything. Accept your circumstances as a part of God's plan to change your life. Ask God to help you respond to difficult people and unpleasant situations as Jesus would. God wants to produce the fruit of the Spirit in your life. Will you cooperate with Him in that life-changing process?

Chapter Three

BECOMING A MORE
LOVING PERSON

First Corinthians 13 ends with these familiar words, "And now these three remain: faith, hope and love. But the greatest of these is love." Love is also the first fruit of the Spirit mentioned in Galatians 5. But what is love?

Love is probably the most misunderstood word in the world. Part of the problem is that we use this one word to describe a lot of things. We water down its meaning by overuse. I love my wife. I love America. I love pizza. I love my dog. I love you. I'd love to have my back rubbed. We use the word *love* in so many different ways that it has, literally, lost its meaning.

It's difficult to give or receive love when you don't even understand what it is. Now, we need to clear up a couple of popular misconceptions about love. Most people think love is a feeling. It's a sentimental knot in your stomach. A quiver in your liver. An ocean of emotion. True, love does produce feelings, but it is more than a feeling.

In a "Peanuts" cartoon, Charlie Brown and Linus are talking, and Linus says, "She was so cute. I used to see her in Sunday School every week. I used to just sit there and stare at her, and sometimes she'd smile at me. Now I hear she's switched churches."

Charlie Brown looks up and says, "That'll change your theology in a hurry!"

How often we rely on our feelings, and let our feelings motivate us to do all kinds of things we might not normally do. As I said, love produces feelings, some very powerful ones, but it is more than a feeling.

Another misconception is that love is uncontrollable. Have you ever said, "I *fell* in love"—as if you had tripped? We just assume that love can't be controlled. "I can't help it if I'm in love. I can't help myself; I'm in love." Or the opposite: "I can't help myself; I just don't love him anymore." We talk as if love is uncontrollable, but the Bible says love is controllable. In fact, Jesus *commanded* that we love others. His words indicate that we do have control over whom we love and whom we don't love.

Love is a matter of two things: First, love is a matter of choice. The Bible says, "Over all these virtues put on love, which binds them all together in perfect unity" (Col. 3:14). Notice those two little words, *put on*. Love is something we can choose to have. If it were a feeling, we couldn't command it. But we can command a choice. And love is a choice. It is controllable.

The Bible also says that love is a matter of conduct. Love is something we do. It is an action, not a feeling. The Apostle John expressed it this way: "Let us not love with words or tongue but with actions and in truth" (1 John 3:18). Too often we love with words or tongue but not with actions. A young man said to his fiancée, "I love you so much I would die for you, my love." She replied, "Oh, Harold, you're always saying that but you never do it."

Love is more than words. It's more than feelings. Unlike us, the Greeks had four words to differentiate different types of love: *storge*, which means natural affection; *eros*, which means sexual attraction; *philia*, which means emotional affection or friendship; and *agape*, which means unconditional, giving, sacrificial love. When the Bible speaks of God's love for us and the kind of love we're to have for Him and for other people, the word is always *agape*. It's a commitment to act.

Do you know it's possible to love someone you don't even like? Remember I said in chapter 2 that in order for God to teach us to love, He puts us around some unlovely people. It's easy to love people who are kind and lovely, but if God is going to teach us to love, He'll bring some hard-to-love people into our lives. Now the fact is that our lives are full of people we don't like. We don't like the way some people talk. We don't like the way they act. We don't like the way they dress. But most of all, we tend not to like people who don't like us. I once heard a story about Lady Astor, who did not like Winston Churchill. One day she said, "Winston, if you were my husband I'd put arsenic in your tea."

Churchill replied, "Madam, if you were my wife, I'd drink it!"

If you were to think for sixty seconds, you could probably come up with a list of people you don't like. They would probably be people that you have trouble getting along with. Everyone is hard to love some of the time, even you, but some people are hard to love all of the time.

Jesus never demanded that we have a warm affection for everyone. He didn't have warm emotions for the Pharisees. We don't have to like everyone (isn't that a relief?), but we do have to love them. Well, how do we do that?

The Bible tells us there are five steps we need to take to learn to love people. I'm convinced we can learn to love anyone if we will take these steps.

Before I show you how to genuinely love others, I want you to picture in your mind that person you find hard to love—an obnoxious relative, a troublesome neighbor, or a disagreeable coworker. How can you learn to love this kind of a person? Here are five steps.

Experience God's Love
First, before we can love others, we must feel and understand how deeply God loves us. We read in Ephesians: "I pray that Christ will be more and more at home in your hearts, living

within you as you trust in Him. May your roots go down deep into the soil of God's marvelous love; and may you be able to *feel* and *understand*, as all God's children should, how long, how wide, how deep, and how high His love really is; and to *experience* this love for yourselves" (Eph. 3:17-18, TLB, emphasis added).

Circle the words *feel, understand,* and *experience* in that passage. God wants us to feel His love, and He wants us to understand His love. Why? First John 4:19 states that we love because God first loved us. Why is it important to feel loved by God? Because unloved people are often unloving people. When I don't feel genuinely loved, I don't feel like giving love. So first we've got to experience God's love ourselves. Jesus said, "Love each other as I have loved you" (John 15:12). That's the model.

Forgive Your Enemies
The second step in learning to love others is forgiving those who have hurt us. Colossians 3:13 says, "Forgive whatever grievances you may have against one another. Forgive as the Lord forgave you." It is impossible to love anyone fully and at the same time resent someone else. I cannot really love my wife if I'm still angry at my parents. I cannot love my child if I'm still angry at my brother. You cannot give total love when your heart is divided. And a bitter heart is a divided heart.

Now you may be thinking, "I can't love my spouse. He's a wonderful person, but I just can't love him." You are probably still reacting to your past and harboring resentment against someone. That is what is keeping you from loving your spouse. And it's not fair. It's not fair to your spouse.

Many people have a just cause for their anger. (I recently heard a news report on the radio that one out of every three women and one out of every seven men will be abused during their lifetime.) But we have to let go of the past to get on with the present. In order to begin loving people today, we must close the door on the past. And there is only one way to do it—forgiveness! Forgive those who have hurt you, for your sake not because they deserve it. Do it so your heart can be whole again. The people from your past cannot continue to hurt you today unless you allow them to hurt you by holding onto resentment against them.

Anytime you resent someone, you give him a piece of your heart. You give him a piece of your attention, a piece of your mind. Do you want him to have a piece? No. So take it back by forgiving. Forgive those who hurt you. Instead of rehearsing that hurt over and over, release it.

Think Loving Thoughts

The next step in learning to love others is to think loving thoughts. God's Word reminds us: "Don't just think about your own affairs, but be interested in others, too, and in what they are doing. Your attitude should be the kind that was shown us by Jesus Christ" (Phil. 2:4-5, TLB). Now, what does it mean to think loving thoughts? It means we begin to focus on other people's needs, hurts, problems, desires, and goals, not just on our own. It's easier to understand someone else when we walk a mile in their moccasins, as the old saying goes. Here is a fact of life: Hurt people hurt people. If someone is hurting you, he's acting this way because he is hurting. Hurt people hurt others. What we need to do is look beyond people's faults and see their needs. Then we can learn to love.

Haven't you found it to be true that the most obnoxious people and the least lovable people are those who *need* love the most? The people you would rather ignore are the very ones who desperately need massive doses of love. Everyone needs love. If a person can't get love, he'll strive for attention. And if he can't get positive attention, he'll work at attracting negative attention. Subconsciously, he is saying, "I will be noticed, one way or another."

In chapter 2 we noted that our thoughts determine our emotions. We cannot change our feelings, but we can go in the back door and change our thoughts. When we change the way we think about someone, we will gradually change our feelings about him. And if instead of thinking about a person's faults we begin to think about his needs, it will change the way we feel. Try it and see for yourself!

Act in Love

The fourth step in learning to love others is to act in a loving way. You say, "Rick, you're telling me to act lovingly toward somebody I don't even like. I couldn't do that. I'd be a hypocrite." No, that's called loving by faith. When you love by faith, you act yourself into a feeling.

This is an important point. It is easier to act my way into a feeling than to feel my way into an action. If I act as if I am enthusiastic, I'll soon begin to feel enthusiastic. If I act as if I am happy, before you know it I'll feel happy. Try this right now. Put the biggest smile on your face that you can muster up. Then make yourself laugh—really laugh from inside yourself. At first it will seem forced, but dig deep and create the body movement of laughter. You'll begin to feel happier. If we begin to act lovingly, we'll soon feel loving.

Not only do our actions influence our emotions but, as I mentioned earlier, our thinking also influences the way we feel. We can attack feelings from either side—or better yet, from both sides.

Change Your Feelings Indirectly

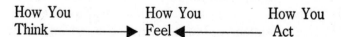

| How You
Think | ⟶ | How You
Feel | ◀ | How You
Act |

If you say, "I can't change my feelings," you are focusing directly on your feelings. You can't change your feelings directly, but you can change them indirectly by changing your thoughts *and* your actions.

Now, how do I act in a loving way? Jesus gives us some help in Luke 6:27-28: "Love your enemies, do good to those who hate you, bless those who curse you, pray for those who mistreat you." He commands us to do four specific things.

First, He says to love our enemies. How do you love someone who is hurting you? You must overlook his faults. Ephesians 4:2 says, "Be patient with each other, making allowance for each other's faults because of your love" (TLB).

Then Jesus also commands us to "Do good." How do you do good to people you don't even like? You look for ways to give to them. What can you do to serve them, to meet their needs, to help them, to benefit them? You can give. You can go the second mile. You can offer practical help. You can do them a favor. You can discover their real needs and respond to those needs.

Jesus also says to bless those who curse us. What does He mean by that? He's referring to the way you talk *about* them, and the way you talk *to* them. A blessing is a positive word spoken to or about others. You don't put them down, you lift them up. You encourage them. Proverbs 12:18 says, "The tongue of the wise brings healing."

Finally, Jesus commands us to pray for those who mistreat us. Praying for people will not only change them, but it will also change us. Now, how do we pray? We pray that God will bless these people who are mistreating us because we know that the goodness of God leads to repentance. Perhaps God will bless these people so much that they will want to change. But even if they don't change right away, praying for them will change our attitude toward them.

So you see, love is an action. First Corinthians 13 says that love is patient, kind, and much more. Fifteen actions are listed in verses 4 to 8. When you act lovingly—when you are patient or gentle or kind—you are displaying the fruit of the Spirit. Love is not simply the first fruit mentioned, it is actually *the* fruit. All the others are simply expressions of love. Love is patient. Love is kind. Love is joyful. Love is the basis of all positive actions.

First, you must understand that God loves you. Then you begin to feel it, not just intellectually, but in your heart. Then you forgive those who have hurt you in the past in order to free yourself of the past so you can love today. Then you start thinking loving thoughts and acting in loving ways, and the feelings will start coming.

Expect the Best

The last step in learning to love others may be the most difficult in some ways: expect the best of them. That person you don't even like, expect the best of him. First Corinthians 13:7 says, "If you love someone . . . you will always believe in him, always expect the best of him" (TLB). Notice the words *expect the best*. Love expects the best. Have you discovered that we tend to live up to what people expect of us? The father who always says to his son, "You'll never amount to anything; you're just a dunce," is setting the boy up for failure. When we expect the best, we bring out the best. This is loving by faith. And loving by faith is the greatest force in the world. Love is contagious, and it changes people. It can transform a personality!

You may be thinking, "Well, I'd like to change my mate." Do you want to know how to change your mate? I can give you the secret in one sentence. This is how you change anyone—your children, your mate, a coworker—Treat them the way you want them to become. Do you want your mate to succeed? Treat him or her like a successful person. Do you want your children to be smart? Treat them as if they are intelligent, not stupid. Treat them the way you want them to become. Don't do this as an act of manipulation but because you genuinely believe in them. Love expects the best.

Now you may be thinking, *Well, I'm stuck in a marriage that is dead or dying. There's just no spark left. Once there was love, but there's no love now. Once there were feelings, but there aren't any now.* Perhaps you've heard that painful statement: "I don't love you anymore." What do you do about that? Do you end the marriage? No, you ask God to resurrect those feelings of love.

Experience God's Resurrection Power

In chapter 1 we talked about resurrection power. This power raised Jesus from the dead, and it can also raise a dead relationship. How do you rekindle a lost love?

"Can I ever learn to love my mate again? Can I ever have those feelings that I used to have when we were dating? Can I ever recapture those feelings?"

Yes, you can.

"But they're dead and gone. I have no feeling anymore."

You can have those feelings back if you choose to have them. Not by saying, "I'm going to force myself to feel loving." That won't work. You can't force a feeling. You can't force the spark back into a relationship, but you can attack the problem indirectly by thinking and acting lovingly. Your thoughts and actions will produce the loving feelings.

In Revelation 2, Christ speaks to the church at Ephesus. He talks to them about a love they had lost—their love for God. That love had become dry and passionless as they merely went through the motions of their commitment to God. Jesus told them to take three steps to rekindle that love. These steps may also be powerfully applied to the rekindling of any relationship. Jesus says, *"Remember the height from which you* have fallen! *Repent* and *do* the things you did at first" (Rev. 2:4-5, emphasis added).

The first step in resurrecting love is to *remember:* "Remember the height from which you have fallen" (v. 5). Rekindling a lost love in your marriage starts with thinking about how you used to love your mate. Remember the happy times. Recall the qualities that first captured your heart. You must choose to remember the experiences you have shared together—the events that have brought you close. Maybe it was while you were dating. Maybe it was early in your marriage. Maybe it was the birth of a child or the purchase of your first home. Whatever it was, start remembering those things. Don't recall the bad things. Those are easy to remember. Instead, choose to focus on the good things that have happened in your relationship.

The second step Jesus tells us to take in resurrecting love is to *repent.* The word *repent* comes from the Greek word, *metanoia,* which means to change your mind, to change the way you think. So when Jesus calls you to repent, He calls you to start changing the way you think about that person you've lost your love for. Stop fantasizing about what might have been. Stop daydreaming about what life might be like if you were married to somebody else. Stop thinking about what life might be like if your mate were different or had done this or that. Stop torturing yourself with "What if?" You're talking yourself into those unhappy feelings. Stop fantasizing and start thinking positive, truthful thoughts, the kind described in 1 Corinthians 13. If you want to rebuild a love in your life, memorize 1 Corinthians 13. Meditate on it and start acting on it.

The third step Jesus tells us to take in resurrecting love is to *do the things you did at first.* Love takes action. You have to work at loving your mate—as hard and creatively as you did during your courtship and engagement. Do the things you did at the start. Perhaps you haven't had a romantic evening in months, maybe years. It may be that you haven't even had time alone together in months. Take time to go out on a date and do the things—buy the flowers, wear that special dress—just like you did at first. Let your creativity come alive again.

Stop fantasizing about greener grass somewhere else. The truth is the grass is not greener on that side of the fence, and it is also not greener on this side of the fence. The grass is greener where you water it! If you will take the energy you spend complaining and fantasizing and invest it in improving your marriage, you'll have a great marriage. You'll rekindle those lost feelings, no matter how long it has been since you last felt them. Love works if you work at it.

If you can identify with this problem of trying to resurrect a dying love, I want to challenge you to do two things. First, commit yourself totally to Jesus Christ. Frankly, I don't have much hope for marriages that aren't based on a commitment to Jesus Christ. All the pressures of today's culture are working against your marriage. I think the divorce statistics bear me out on this. The fact is, human love is not strong enough to weather the storms of life. Human love dries up. But *agape,* God's love, never gives up.

The root of your problem is spiritual. It's not an emotional problem or a relational problem. Your relationship with God affects your relationship with your spouse and everyone else. When you're not right with God, you're not going to be right with other people either. The vertical and the horizontal planes must be in balance. Each affects the other. The starting point is to correct your vertical relationship to God and then your horizontal relationship with others will be easier to correct.

The Holy Spirit can fill you with new reservoirs of love you never thought you could have. You need God's love, God's power. So commit your life totally and unreservedly to Jesus Christ.

The second thing you must do to rekindle your marriage is commit yourself totally and unreservedly to your mate, regardless of faults and flaws. Don't fall into the *I'd love you if* syndrome: "I'd love you *if* you would pay more attention to me. I'd love you *if* you would do this or that for me." That's conditional love. God's love is the kind that says: "I love you, period. I love you unconditionally." Actually, God's love really says: "I love you in spite of. . . ." He tells us, "I love you in spite of the fact that you are imperfect. I love you in spite of the fact that you have problems. I love you." Now that's *agape* love, the kind of love that makes a difference.

So pray for a resurrection, and choose to do what Jesus says: remember, repent, and take action. When you do that, you'll be surprised how quickly your feelings return.

Chapter Four

THE CHOICE
TO REJOICE!

Everyone wants to be happy. If you ask people what their number one ambition in life is, most people will say, "I just want to be happy." In Orange County, California, where I live, being happy is serious business. I mean, we work at it. It's like no other place in the nation. We have this idea that we must be happy all the time. I must act happy. I must talk happy. I must smell happy. I certainly must look happy. And if I'm not happy, I must fake it. Put on a mask, and remember you're supposed to be having a great time.

Always having to appear happy creates stress. I see a lot more people faking happiness than living reality. The fact is, every day doesn't score a "perfect 10." Everything does not always work out according to the way we planned it. Some days are disasters. Let's be honest about it.

It's a Bad Day When . . .
You know it's going to be a bad day when you call your answering service, and they tell you it's none of your business. You know it's going to be a bad day when your horn goes off suddenly and remains stuck as you follow a group of Hell's Angels on the freeway. And you know it's going to be a bad day when you sink your teeth into a beautiful steak and they stay there.

It's easy to be happy when everything is going our way. But what about the rest of life? Are we only happy when everything is going our way? If so, you're going to be unhappy for much of your life.

How can we stay positive in a negative world? How can we remain optimistic when everything is falling apart? This is where joy comes in. Galatians 5:22 states, "The fruit of the Spirit is . . . joy." And Philippians 4:4 reminds us, "Rejoice in the Lord always. I will say it again: Rejoice!"

Happiness depends on happenings. It comes from the root word *hap*, which means luck or circumstance. "I'm happy today because things just happened to turn out right."

Joy is different. It's deeper. Joy is an attitude, a choice. Joy is an inside job. It's not dependent on circumstances. It is your *choice* to rejoice. This is the basic truth of this chapter. You can choose, regardless of the circumstances, to be joyful.

Joy is what makes life enjoyable. When we learn to choose joy, life will be greatly enhanced. As Christians, we can be the most positive people in the world. Why? Romans 5 gives us three reasons.

We Have Hope

Romans 5 opens with these words: "Therefore, since we have been justified through faith, we have peace with God through our Lord Jesus Christ, through whom we have gained access by faith into this grace in which we now stand" (vv. 1-2). Paul goes on to explain that the result of experiencing the grace of God is that "we rejoice in the hope of the glory of God" (v. 2). For a Christian, no situation is completely hopeless.

It has been said that a person can live forty days without food, three days without water, eight minutes without air, but not one minute without hope. We've got to have hope. Some researchers at Cornell University studied 25,000 prisoners of war from World War II. They concluded that a person can handle almost anything if he has hope.

A lot of people have hope, but they haven't based it on anything solid. It's an artificial, pump-yourself-up hope. And many people base their hope on the wrong things: the stock *steady boyfriend. But I did get a D in French and an F in Chemistry, and I just wanted to be sure you received this news in the proper perspective.*

Perspective makes all the difference in the world. How you respond to problems at work, problems at home, health problems, depends on your perspective. Paul says that as Christians we can rejoice even in tough times because we have hope and because we know that God is working in our lives. We have perspective.

Paul reminds us: "We know that suffering *produces*. . . ." Circle that word. Suffering can be productive! It does accomplish something. Problems have a purpose. Your trials and difficulties have value. It's easier to handle suffering when you know there is a purpose in it, that it is not just in vain.

I have had the privilege of assisting in the delivery of all three of my children. I want to tell you, I've seen the pain on my wife's face in labor. I now know why they call it "labor." But I've also seen the expression on her face when the nurse lays that brand-new, bundled baby in her weary arms. Her expression reveals that the effort and pain were all worth it. They produced a new life!

Now, what exactly does our suffering produce? First, Paul says our suffering produces perseverance (Rom. 5:3). The Greek word for perseverance literally means the ability to handle pressure. That's what perseverance is—the ability to handle pressure, to hang in there, to never give up but to keep on keeping on. When we make it through a difficult time without giving up, our character and confidence are strengthened, enabling us to handle even more pressure when it comes in the future.

Next, Paul says perseverance produces character (Rom. 5:4). This word occurs only six or seven times in the Bible, and it means "proven reliable." It's like the luggage we talked about that's bounced around the room. That luggage has character. It's proven reliable. God wants to make you that kind of person, and He uses suffering to do it. He uses the problems in your life to produce perseverance and character. And internal character, not circumstances, produces joy.

Then, Paul says, character produces hope (Rom. 5:4). Remember that the word *hope,* in the Bible, doesn't mean "I wish," or "I want." It means confidence in Christ's power. Instead of destroying our hope, problems are designed to increase our hope!

No matter what it is, whether it is a problem you brought on yourself, or a problem other people brought on you, or a problem from the devil, it's a problem that God allowed. If you are a Christian, nothing comes into your life by accident.

It's vitally important that we grasp this fact that there is a purpose behind our problems, but it's also important to understand that problems don't automatically produce perseverance and character and hope. You may know people who went through tough times, but difficulty and pain didn't produce any positive character in their lives. Instead they became bitter, angry, and uptight. Perseverance, character, and hope are produced in us only when we *choose* the right attitude. And what is the right attitude? *Joy* is the right attitude. When we learn to rejoice in the problem, not *for* but *in* the problem, then God uses it for good in our lives.

James echoes Paul's teaching on this subject: "Consider it pure joy, my brothers, whenever you face trials of many kinds, because you know that the testing of your faith develops perseverance" (James 1:2-3). Notice again, joy comes "because you know." It's always a matter of perspective. James continues, "Perseverance must finish its work so that you may be mature and complete, not lacking anything" (v. 4). God says those problems in your life are meant to produce maturity.

No study of Christian joy would be complete without mentioning the Book of Philippians. If you want to understand joy, read Philippians. Nineteen times in this short letter Paul talks about rejoicing and having joy. Mark those verses and meditate on them. Memorize some of them so God can use them to produce joy in your life.

By the way, do you know where Paul was when he wrote this joyful letter? He was in prison! We don't usually think of prison as a place of rejoicing, but Paul had learned to be content in any situation, and his joy did not depend on his circumstances. Christians can be joyful in tough times because there is always hope and because God's purpose is always greater than any problem!

He Is with Us
In Romans 5:11, Paul mentions a third reason we can be joyful: "We rejoice because of what God has done through our Lord Jesus Christ, who has now made us God's friends" (GNB). We can be joyful no matter what the circumstances because God is always with those who believe in Him, no matter where we are or what we're facing. As believers, we have been reconciled to God through Jesus Christ. We have become God's friends, and this friendship will last forever.

Take a few minutes right now to meditate on Isaiah 43:2. "When you pass through deep waters, I will be with you; your troubles will not overwhelm you. When you pass through fire, you will not be burned" (GNB).

You may need that verse this week. It's saying that, if you are a believer, God is with you and nothing can overwhelm you. Nothing can destroy you. The devil can't. (He doesn't have enough power.) Other people can't, and God won't. *Nothing can overwhelm you!* No matter what you go through in life, you will never go through it alone. Now *that* is reason to rejoice!

Develop a Spiritual Workout

Let me suggest four exercises that develop inner joy. Joy is like a muscle. The more you exercise it, the stronger it becomes. Do these four things for the next six weeks and see what a difference they make in your life. I guarantee that you will become a more positive, joyful person. It worked in my life ten years ago when I made this decision.

First, develop the attitude of gratitude. First Thessalonians 5:18 says, "Give thanks in all circumstances, for this is God's will for you in Christ Jesus." That's the attitude of gratitude. Notice again that we don't have to be thankful *for* all circumstances, but we are to be thankful *in* all circumstances.

Psychologists say that gratitude is the healthiest emotion. Hans Seyle, the father of stress studies, claimed that gratitude produces more emotional energy than any other attitude in your life. Haven't you found it to be true that the people who are the most grateful are the happiest people you know?

I challenge you to look for ways to express gratitude this week and see what a difference it makes. Maybe write a note expressing appreciation to someone. Or make a phone call to tell someone how much he has meant in your life. And don't forget to express gratitude to God. The psalmist says: "My heart leaps for joy and I will give thanks to Him in song" (Ps. 28:7). If you're not a joyful person, start singing hymns of praise to God and watch your attitude change.

Second, cultivate inner joy by giving. Jesus teaches us that "it is more blessed to give than to receive" (Acts 20:35). Someone has said that when it comes to giving, many people will stop at nothing. What does the Bible say? "God loves a cheerful giver" (2 Cor. 9:7). Why? Perhaps it's because we are most like God when we give, and He does not give grudgingly.

In addition, our giving determines how much God can do in our lives. When we give to Him gladly, we open ourselves to receive from Him freely. In Malachi 3:10 we read: " 'Bring the whole tithe into the storehouse, that there may be food in my house. Test me in this,' says the Lord Almighty, 'and see if I will not throw open the floodgates of heaven and pour out so much blessing that you will not have room enough for it.' " You've heard of the Pepsi Challenge; this is the Heavenly Challenge! We can't outgive God. As the godly old farmer said, "I shovel into God's storehouse and He shovels into mine—and God has a bigger shovel."

The third way to develop inner joy is through service: give your life to helping others. Jesus said we must lose our life in order to save it (Mark 8:35). In the Book of Ephesians, Paul reminds us: "Serve wholeheartedly, as if you were serving the Lord, not men, because you know that the Lord will reward everyone for whatever good he does" (Eph. 6:7-8). The happiest people are usually too busy serving and helping others to ask themselves, "Am I happy?"

Joy comes as we get our focus off ourselves and concentrate on helping others. There are probably lots of areas of service in your church just waiting for someone like you to fill them. Ask your pastor or Sunday School director if you can do something to help out. It will make his day—after he regains consciousness!

The final exercise aimed at developing inner joy is sharing Christ with others. Jesus says there is rejoicing in heaven when a person comes to faith in Christ (Luke 15:10). My greatest joy came when I committed my life to Jesus Christ; my second greatest joy has been to introduce others to Him. Imagine the scene in heaven: Someone you witnessed to comes over to you and says, "I want to thank you for caring and taking the time. I'm here because you cared enough to tell me about Jesus." I tell you, that will be a time of rejoicing. But that's the culmination of the joy; it begins here and now when you assist in the birth of a new child into the family of God.

Every once in a while I run into a Christian who says, "I've lost my joy." The question I want to ask is: "When was the last time you led someone to Christ?" It has usually been a long time. Concerning his fellow Jews, Paul said, "How I wish with all my heart that my own people might be saved! How I pray to God for them!" (Rom. 10:1, GNB) Ask God to give you a burden like that.

Joy is elusive because the very exercises that produce it run counter to what our culture teaches about joy. Our culture says, "Live for yourself and forget about others." But our Lord tells us that joy comes from developing an attitude of gratitude and giving of our material possessions, our time, and our knowledge of the Good News. I challenge you to try these four exercises for six weeks. If you practice them faithfully, I guarantee you'll be a more joyful person. P805

Chapter Five

PEACEFUL LIVING IN AN
UPTIGHT WORLD

Everyone wants peace of mind. Whether you're a businessman facing the pressure of deadlines at the office, a homemaker trying to corral the kids, or a student just trying to make it through the semester, everyone wants peace of mind. But most of us, if we're honest with ourselves, have to admit that we experience more stress than peace.

How familiar are you with stress? Let me give you a little quiz. Complete each of these sentences with the appropriate word:

I'm ready to throw in the. . . .
I'm at the end of my. . . .
I'm just a bundle of. . . .
My life is falling. . . .
I'm at my wit's. . . .
I feel like resigning from the human. . . .

How did you do? If you answered *towel, rope, nerves, apart, end,* and *race* in that order, give yourself an *A* +. You're an expert on the subject of stress! Most of us have muttered these sayings often enough that they are almost second nature.

Stress is an unfortunate fact of life in our modern world. Everyone's under stress. Everyone's tense. Statistics tell us that people in the United States consume 15 tons of aspirin every day. Sales of tranquilizers are at an all-time high. Books on peace of mind become instant best-sellers.

Too much stress is unhealthy, we're told. What else is new? We've known that for centuries. Nearly 3,000 years ago, Solomon wrote, "A heart at peace gives life to the body, but envy rots the bones" (Prov. 14:30). The Bible has a lot to say about stress, and even more about its antidote—peace of mind. But what is peace?

You Need Three Kinds of Peace

The Bible talks about three kinds of peace. First is *spiritual peace*. Spiritual peace is peace *with* God. Romans 5:1 says, "Since we have been justified through faith, we have peace with God through our Lord Jesus Christ." That's the foundation, the bottom line. We've got to have peace with God before we can have any other kind of peace. I hope you have found that peace. There's only one way, and it's through Jesus Christ (John 14:6).

Next comes *emotional peace*. Emotional peace is the peace *of* God. First we must have peace *with* God; that's spiritual peace. Then we can have the peace *of* God; that's emotional peace. This is what most of us think about when we think of the word peace—an internal sense of well-being and order.

Colossians 3:15 says, "Let the peace of Christ rule in your hearts, since . . . you were called to peace." The Greek word translated *rule* here is used only this one time in the Bible and it means "to umpire." This verse says we should let the peace of God be the umpire in our lives. What does an umpire do? He keeps the peace. He makes sure the game is played in a smooth and orderly manner. God wants to give you an internal umpire who will keep you at peace even when everything seems chaotic.

Have you ever heard anyone say, "I need to get away"? Maybe you've said it yourself. Have you ever been so tired at night that your body collapses into the bed but your mind won't turn off? Your mind just races from one thought to another. Well, you *can* get away. You can go to Tahiti today, but if you don't have emotional peace, your mind will still be racing on the beach in Tahiti. You can't run away from yourself. You need both spiritual peace and emotional peace.

Third, you need *relational peace,* or peace with other people. This is what the Bible calls peace *with men.* Romans 12:18 says, "If it is possible, as far as it depends on you, live at peace with everyone." Relational peace reduces conflict.

I'm sure you would agree that relationships can be a source of stress. For most of us, our biggest problems are people problems: getting along with the boss, the family, the relatives. We must deal with conflict and competition and criticism on a regular basis. These things can rob our peace.

How desperately we need spiritual, emotional, and relational peace. But can we really find peace?

Understand the Promise of God's Peace

Look at what Jesus promised us in John 14:27: "I leave behind with you—peace; I give you My own peace and My gift is nothing like the peace of this world. You must not be distressed and you must not be daunted" (PH). He spoke these words right before He went to the cross.

Notice that Jesus says His peace is a gift. We can't work for it, and we can't earn it. We can't psych ourselves up for it. We can't try really hard to get it. It's a gift we simply accept.

He also says His peace is different from what the world gives. The world's peace is a fragile peace. How many cease-fires have we had in Lebanon in the last few years? Someone has figured out that in the last 3,500 years the world has had 286 years of peace. The peace of the world is temporary.

Finally, God's peace is not related to circumstances. God's peace allows us to be tranquil in the midst of trouble. Now, how do we get this peace? Following are five keys to acquiring God's perfect peace.

Obey God's Principles

First, if we want peace, we must obey God's principles found in His Word. Just do what the Bible says. The psalmist says, "Great peace have they who love Your law, and nothing can make them stumble. . . . I obey Your statutes, for I love them greatly" (Ps. 119:165, 167). God says peace comes when we live in harmony with Him—when we do what He tells us to do.

I bought a car recently. In the glove compartment of a new car there is an owner's manual. This owner's manual tells me that if I do certain things at certain times, I'll get more mileage out of my car.

God's Word is your owner's manual for life. It contains principles for health, finance, marriage, relationships, business, and much more. You may ignore these principles, but if you do, you don't have anybody to blame for your problems but yourself. If you don't obey these principles, you will not experience peace. Just as a car runs more smoothly when you operate it according to its design, your life will run more smoothly if you live it according to God's design as presented in His Word. It's that simple. If you want to be at peace, obey God's principles.

Accept God's Pardon

Next, if we want peace, we must accept God's pardon. What does it mean to pardon? It means to release from punishment. It means to forgive.

Guilt is the number one destroyer of peace for most people. When we feel guilty, we feel we're being haunted and chased by our past. What if someone finds out? What if someone sees the skeleton in the closet? That's why we read in newspapers about people who, thirty years after the fact, make restitution for a wrong they committed way back when. They say, "I was living in hell for thirty years and had to get it off my chest." The only way to have peace of mind is to have a clear conscience, and only God can give that.

Micah 7:18 says, "Who is a God like you, who pardons sin and forgives the transgressions. . . . You do not stay angry forever but delight to show mercy." Notice that Micah says God is eager—willing and waiting—to clean your slate. It's His nature. He likes to forgive. Someone has said that God has a big eraser. God's Word tells us: "If we confess our sins, He is faithful and just and will forgive us our sins" (1 John 1:9). God's forgiveness is available, so if you don't have a clear conscience, get one today.

Focus on God's Presence

If we want peace, we must focus on God's presence. We must realize that God is always with us, and we must learn to sense His presence. Isaiah 26:3 reminds us to fix our gaze on God: "You will keep in perfect peace him whose mind is steadfast, because he trusts in You." We have a choice of either focusing on our problems or focusing on God, who holds the solution. Corrie ten Boom, author of *The Hiding Place*, wrote: "The blacker the night around us grew, the brighter and truer and more beautiful burned the Word of God" (Guideposts Associates, Inc., p. 177). If you look at the world, you'll be distressed; if you look within, you'll be depressed; but if you look at Christ, you'll be at rest. It's what you concentrate on that determines your level of personal peace. Focus on God's presence; He is with you, and He has promised He will never leave you.

On Friday afternoons in our church office we sometimes do silly things. One Friday afternoon we were playing around with stress dots. Do you know what stress dots are? James Dobson talked about them on his radio program, so we wrote in and got a set. They are little pressure-sensitive dots that you put on your hand. As adrenaline changes in your system, the dots change color and show you if you are under stress. We were experimenting with them to see if we could affect each other's stress level. I remember saying, "Wouldn't it be great if we had a little internal warning light that told us whenever our focus was off the Lord. Or if we had a little beep or signal light that told us we were not in tune with God?" Then I realized we do have a warning light! It's called tension, or stress. Becoming tense is a clear indication that we have taken our eyes off the Lord and placed them on circumstances. We're looking at the problem rather than the solution. Now, when you look at a problem, you're going to get tense. But try to remember that stress is God's way of saying, "Get your focus in order: look at Me."

The psalmist says, "God is our refuge and strength, an ever-present help in trouble" (Ps. 46:1). Later in the same chapter he reminds us, "Be still, and know that I am God" (Ps. 46:10). These verses have an interesting background. They were not written by David; this psalm was written during the time of Hezekiah many years after David lived. The nation of Israel was under attack from Sennacherib, the king of Assyria. Enemy soldiers had surrounded Jerusalem, and the Israelites were uptight. They knew they were going to get it, so they prayed this prayer. Five minutes before noon, God smote the Assyrians with a plague and 185,000 of them died. Jerusalem was saved and everyone was happy. That's the background of this psalm. That reminds us God is our refuge; He's our strength no matter how overwhelming the odds seem. He is an ever-present help in time of trouble!

This psalm tells us two things about getting God's help in a time of trouble. The first thing is to *be still* when we are in trouble. The Hebrew word there means to ease up, to let go. It's been said that most of our problems come from our inability to sit still. When was the last time you just sat still and focused on the Lord? Try it right now. Take a deep breath, let it out, and focus on God's presence surrounding you. Do that

50 to 60 times a day, whenever you feel the tension building. Take mini-vacations in your mind. Be still. Hurry is the death of prayer.

In addition to telling us to be still, the Lord reminds us: *"Know that I am God."* Did you know that right in the middle of a hurricane or tornado is a quiet center, called an eye? Likewise, even though everything is blowing apart around you, there can be a quiet center in your life. *Be still* and *know.* Obey God's principles, accept God's pardon, focus on God's presence, "and the peace of God that passes all understanding will guard your hearts and minds in Christ Jesus" (Phil. 4:7).

Trust God's Purpose
If we want to experience God's peace, we must trust God's purpose. Even when things don't make sense, we must trust God's purpose. Listen to what Proverbs 3:5-6 says: "Trust in the Lord with all your heart, and lean not on your own under-standing; in all your ways acknowledge Him and He shall direct your paths" (NKJV). How many verbs do you see in these verses? There are four of them. The first one is *trust.* It is followed by *lean not, acknowledge,* and *direct.* The first three verbs are used as commands: trust, lean not, and acknowledge. The fourth verb is used to express a promise. God says, "I will direct your paths."

Let's consider trust for a minute. Have you noticed that a lot of things in life don't make sense? And do you feel that a lot of things in life are beyond your control? What do you do in such situations? You trust! That's really all you can do. "Lean not" says the same thing. Don't try to figure life out yourself. We do that all the time, don't we? We waste a lot of time and energy always trying to figure things out. God urges us to just trust Him.

Most people worry about two common problems: illness and death. We all face illness, and we all will die someday. How can I have peace when a loved one is terminally ill? How should I respond when a friend dies unexpectedly? God tells me to trust Him, not try to figure it out by myself.

I've had people tell me on more than a few occasions that when they finally stopped trying to figure out why God allowed something to happen and just started trusting Him, then the peace came. We need to face the fact that not all of our questions are going to be answered in this lifetime.

One of the lessons I'm learning slowly is that I don't have to understand *why* or *how* or even *when* God does what He does; all I have to do is trust Him in order to experience His peace. As long as I'm struggling to figure things out, I'm not really trusting God and I probably won't have peace. We have to trust God with our lives and with the lives of our loved ones.

The writer of Proverbs urges us to trust God and not depend on our own understanding. Then he reminds us to acknowledge God. Now, what does it mean to acknowledge God? It means to recognize and accept the fact that God is sovereignly in control of the universe, including the part of the universe you and I inhabit. We must acknowledge that God is in control and that He doesn't make mistakes. Someday I am going to preach a sermon on words or phrases we'll never hear God say. One of the words is *Oops*. God never has to say, "Oops," because He never makes a mistake. Everything that happens in your life fits into God's plan for you. He uses every situation, even the problems and heartaches and difficulties you bring on yourself, to work out His purpose in your life. He fits everything perfectly into His plan and purpose for you. All God expects from you is that you trust Him without trying to figure it all out. Acknowledge that God is in control.

When you do this, you have His promise that He will "direct" your life or, as the NIV puts it, "He will make your paths straight" (Prov. 3:6). Many of us, when we try to direct our own lives, follow haphazard paths filled with indecision:

"Should I do this or do that? Should I go here or go there?" Indecision produces stress. But when we trust in the Lord, He directs our paths, and He makes them straight, not stressful.

The Apostle Paul learned this lesson. He was at peace because He knew God was directing his life. Even when he was locked in a Roman prison, he could write, "I have learned the secret of being content in any and every situation, whether well fed or hungry, whether living in plenty or in want" (Phil. 4:12). Then he tells us the "secret" he has learned: "I can do everything through Him who gives me strength" (4:13). Notice here that this was something Paul had to *learn;* it didn't come naturally to him any more than it does to us. He *learned* to trust the Lord and to allow Him to direct his life—and he was content; he was at peace. The safest, most serene place to be is in the center of God's will.

One of my favorite scenes in the Bible is when Jesus and the disciples are in a fishing boat on the Sea of Galilee and a storm comes up. Do you remember the story? It's found in Luke 8:22-25 if you'd like to review the details. What fascinates me is that Jesus could sleep right through that raging storm. We know the storm was severe because of the disciples' reaction to it. Remember, a number of them were experienced fishermen; they had been through many storms before. But they didn't think they would make it through this one. In the midst of this storm and all the commotion on the boat, Jesus was sound asleep. How could He sleep? Because He knew something the disciples didn't know—He knew everything was under control. It didn't look like it was, but with one word from Jesus the storm subsided.

Peter learned something from that incident about getting a good night's sleep. Some years later, he was arrested by King Herod and put in prison to await execution. The night before Peter was to be killed, God sent an angel to rescue him. We read about it in Acts 12. Notice that the angel had to strike

Peter on the side to wake him up (v. 7). Peter was sleeping like a baby! Why? Because he was trusting the Lord who was directing his life. That's peace, real peace!

Ask for God's Peace

If we want God's peace, we need to ask for it. Again in Philippians 4, Paul tells us, "Do not be anxious about anything, but in everything, by prayer and petition, with thanksgiving, present your requests to God. And the *peace of God,* which transcends all understanding, will guard your hearts and your minds in Christ Jesus" (vv. 6-7, emphasis added). Notice the order—first prayer and then peace. There's a cause and effect relationship here. Prayer is the cause; peace is the effect.

If you're not praying, you're likely to be worrying. And worry is such a useless emotion, such a waste. Worry is the opposite of peace; they cannot coexist. Our word *worry* comes from the German word *wergen,* which means "to choke." That's what worry does; it chokes your life. Jesus said so in explaining the Parable of the Sower in Luke 8. Look at His words: "The seed that fell among thorns stands for those who hear, but as they go on their way they are choked by life's worries, riches and pleasures, and they do not mature" (v. 14). Do you see it? "Choked by life's worries."

When the pressure builds up, don't panic . . . pray! Prayer is a tremendous stress reliever. It can be your safety valve. When the pressure builds up within you and you feel like you're about to explode, open the safety valve of prayer. Turn your cares into prayers.

I attended a stress management seminar some time back and one of the things I learned is that everyone needs an unconditional listener to unload on. "Talk to your pet," was one of the suggestions. The principle is a valid one: we need an unconditional listener to unload on, one who will not become stressed out by our dumping on him—one who will not think any less of us because of what we say. But a heart-to-heart talk with a hamster is not God's ideal. Who better than God to "dump" on? In fact, Peter uses this image when he says, "Cast all your anxiety on Him because He cares for you" (1 Peter 5:7). Lay it on the Lord! God will not be "stressed out" by what you tell Him. He already knows everything about you and loves you anyway. The seminar teacher had the right idea; he just didn't know the right Person to talk to. Prayer, after all, is talking with God. Tell Him what's on your mind, what's troubling you, and acknowledge His control of the universe, including your life. Ask Him to meet your needs. He can do that better than a whole herd of hamsters.

"Do not let your hearts be troubled," Jesus told His disciples. "Trust in God; trust also in Me" (John 14:1). You will not experience true or lasting peace until Jesus Christ is in charge of your life. Peace, remember, is not a trouble-free life; it's a sense of calm in the midst of life's storms.

What is robbing you of peace today? Is it guilt? Turn to God for forgiveness. Is it worry? A job change? Finances? Major surgery? A difficult person? You can talk to Christ about all of these things and anything else that's bothering you. You'll feel better for having done so and, remember, He can do something about them!

What is your deepest fear? Loneliness? Fear of failure? Death? Illness? Change? Responsibility? Pray this familiar prayer, called the Serenity Prayer: "God, grant me the serenity to accept the things I cannot change, the courage to change the things I can, and the wisdom to know the difference."

The wonderful by-product of your prayer will be peace.

DEVELOPING
YOUR PATIENCE

John Dewey said that the most useful virtue in the world is patience. The fact is, we need it all the time, and we need it everywhere. Proverbs 16:32 says, "It is better to be patient than powerful. It is better to win control over yourself than over whole cities" (GNB).

Years ago, while going through a difficult time, I began praying, "Lord, give me more patience." I expected my problems to decrease, but they got worse! Then I said, "Lord, give me more patience," and the problems got really bad! Later I realized that God had indeed answered my prayer. I had become much more patient, thanks to the problems.

By "testing" our patience God gives us true patience. It's easy to appear patient when everything's going your way. But what happens when things aren't going your way? Perhaps you're like the person who prayed, "Lord, give me patience, and I want it right now!"

A "Peanuts" cartoon begins by showing Lucy praying at her bedside. Then she gets up, walks out, and says to Linus, "I was praying for greater patience and understanding but I quit." Then in the last frame she says, "I was afraid I might get it."

Are you afraid to pray for patience for fear you might get it? How patient are you? Here are four ways to test your patience.

Test Your Patience

The first test is *interruptions.* You know what I mean. You sit down to dinner and the phone rings. Or you're in the bathtub and a salesman comes to the door. Or you're working on a deadline and visitors arrive. Our best plans are often interrupted.

Do you have to deal with interruptions at work? Take heart. Johannes Brahms, when writing his "Lullaby," had so many interruptions in his life that it took him seven years to compose the lullaby. Some people think he just kept falling asleep at the piano.

Even the disciples were impatient with people who interrupted Jesus' schedule (Matt. 19:13-14). They said, "No, don't bring your kids to Jesus now. The Master's busy" (author's paraphrase).

How do you handle interruptions? That's the first test of your patience.

Inconveniences are the second test of your patience. How do you deal with inconveniences in your life? Americans hate to be delayed. We're the "Now Generation." We have a microwave mentality. We want what we want in seconds. We have minute rice, instant coffee, and fast food. We don't like to wait.

We want our information on the spot too; we like up-to-date reports. At election time, pollsters report election results before we have even voted. A hundred years ago people didn't worry if they missed a stagecoach. They could always catch another one in a day or two. Today we have a heart attack if we miss a revolving door! We're in such a hurry. We've got to get going. We can't wait!

In Luke 10:40 we read about a woman who had trouble being patient in the face of inconvenience. Jesus is at the home of Mary and Martha, and Martha is busily preparing the meal. Martha is upset with Mary because Mary has left her to do all the work. You can hear the edge in her voice as she says to Jesus, "Lord, don't You care that my sister has left me to do the work by myself? Tell her to help me!" Maybe you feel this way. Maybe you're carrying that extra load, and you feel put upon and inconvenienced. You'd like to be sitting at Jesus' feet too, but there's work to be done and you're the only one who seems to be aware of it. How do you react? Are you patient despite the inconvenience?

The third test of your patience is *irritations*—those little things in life that bug you. How do you handle them? Here's a list of some irritations I've heard about in the last month: traffic jams, long lines, phone calls, misplaced keys, cold food, late planes, flat tires, occupied bathrooms, neighborhood rock groups. You can make your own list I'm sure. Some of these irritations are controllable, but most of them aren't. So we have to learn to cope. That takes patience.

Moses was irritated with the Israelites on the occasion recorded in Numbers 20:10-11. He had put up with their petty complaints and criticisms for years, and now he had no patience left. When God told him to speak to the rock to get water, he struck it in anger instead. His impatience caused him to disobey God. As a result, God did not allow Moses to enter the Promised Land. Moses was usually a patient person, but even patient people have their limits, or so it would seem.

The Encyclopedia Britannica's 1982 Yearbook, under the heading "Strange and Unusual Events," tells about a man named Brian Heise:

> Brian Heise had more than his share of luck in July, and most of it was bad. When his apartment in Provo, Utah, became flooded from a broken pipe in the upstairs apartment, the manager told him to go out and rent a water vacuum. That's when he discovered his car had a flat tire. He changed it, then went inside again to phone a friend for help. The electric shock he got from the phone so startled him that he inadvertently ripped the instrument off the wall. Before he could

leave the apartment a second time, a neighbor had to kick down the apartment door because water damage had jammed it tight. While all of this was going on, someone stole Heise's car, but it was almost out of gas. He found it a few blocks away but had to push it to the gas station, where he filled up the tank. That evening Heise attended a military ceremony at Brigham Young University. He injured himself severely when he somehow sat on his bayonet, which had been tossed onto the front seat of his car. Doctors were able to stitch up the wound, but no one was able to resuscitate four of Heise's canaries that were crushed to death by falling plaster. After Heise slipped on the wet carpet and badly injured his tailbone, he said he began to wonder if "God wanted me dead, but just kept missing."

And you think you've had bad days!

For many of us, our greatest irritations in life are people. Perhaps you feel like the taxi driver in New York who said, "You know, it's not just the work that I enjoy, but it's the people I run into."

We all run into people who are irritations or who get us down. We must learn the lesson of the oyster. The oyster takes an irritation, a grain of sand, and turns it into a pearl. Learning to respond to irritations positively will enable you to transform your irritations into pearls.

The fourth test of your patience is *inactivity*. Most of us would rather do anything except wait. We hate to wait in the doctor's office, or stand in line at the supermarket, or be confined to bed rest.

Did you know that you will spend six months of your life sitting at red lights waiting for them to turn green? And have you noticed that when the light turns green, if you don't move in two seconds, the guy behind you turns red? Isn't it interesting how we admire patience in the driver who is behind us, but not in the one who is ahead of us? How do you handle inactivity?

You can learn a lot about people by watching how they wait for an elevator to come to their floor. Some people are swayers; they kind of sway back and forth. Some people are bouncers. They bounce up and down while waiting for the elevator to begin moving. Some people are pushers. They're always pushing the button, as if that's going to make the elevator come any faster. They just can't stand and wait. They've got to do something to feel like they're in control.

Job is an example of a man who could do nothing but wait. (We often speak of "the patience of Job.") He said, "All the days of my hard service I will wait for my renewal to come" (Job 14:14). We can learn much from Job's example.

The Bible says, "Impatience will get you into trouble" (Prov. 19:2, GNB). Medical researchers agree with that. They have discovered a whole new disease called "hurry sickness." Drs. Rosenman and Freedman say that 90 percent of heart attack victims have this "hurried" Type A personality. Their habitual impatience gets them into trouble.

Now, what causes impatience? A lack of peace. Perhaps that's why God puts *patience* right after *peace* in the list of the Spirit's fruit. When you have peace in your heart, almost nothing can make you impatient. But when you don't have peace in your heart, almost anything can make you impatient. So how can I learn to be a patient person? The Bible reveals a four-part answer.

Develop a New Perspective
First, develop a new perspective. Find a new way of looking at the situation or the person that is giving you problems. Pa-

tience begins by changing the way you look at something. When I'm impatient, I have a limited perspective. All I'm seeing is myself: *my* needs, *my* desires, *my* goals, *my* wants, *my* schedule, and how you're messing up *my* life. The root of impatience is selfishness. So I need to get a new perspective on life. I need to learn to see things from other people's point of view.

Would you like to know the secret of success? Here it is. If you want to be a successful husband or wife, learn to see life from your partner's point of view. If you want to be a successful parent, learn to see life from your child's point of view. If you want to be a successful businessman, learn to see life from your customers' point of view. If you want to be a successful employer, learn to see life from your employees' point of view. Look at the situation from their perspective and discover why they feel the way they do. I don't know of anything that has greater potential for reducing conflict in your life.

Now look at what the Bible says in the Book of Proverbs. The writer explains: "A man's wisdom gives him patience; it is to his glory to overlook an offense" (Prov. 19:11). Notice the word *wisdom*. Do you know what wisdom is? Wisdom is seeing life from God's point of view, getting God's perspective on the situation. From that perspective I gain three important insights: (1) I'm only human; I'm not God. Of course God knows that. But He wants me to acknowledge it also. I'm not perfect and I'm not in control. In fact, most of the things I face in life are things I can't control. I'm only human. (2) Nobody else is perfect either, so I shouldn't be surprised or overly upset when people make mistakes or let me down. (3) God *is* in control, and He can use the situations, the irritations, and the problems that come into my life to accomplish His purposes for me.

Another verse in Proverbs declares: "A man's steps are directed by the LORD" (Prov. 20:24). This means you may experience some divine delays, some heavenly interruptions. Sometimes the Lord will put irritating people around you for the purpose of teaching you something. Get a new perspective. Look at it from God's point of view.

All through the Bible, God equates patience with maturity. Proverbs 14:29 tells us, "A patient man has great understanding, but a quick-tempered man displays folly." Patience is a mark of maturity. Most children are very impatient; they don't know the difference between "No" and "Not yet." Have you noticed that when babies don't get what they want immediately, they get very upset? Maturity involves the ability to wait, to live with delayed gratification. A man of understanding and wisdom, who sees life from God's point of view, can be patient. So we need to discover a new perspective.

Acquire a Sense of Humor

A second way to become a patient person is to develop a sense of humor. Learn to laugh at your circumstances. Learn to laugh at yourself. Somehow find the fun in the frustrating. Proverbs 14:30 says, "A relaxed attitude lengthens a man's life" (TLB).

I recently read about a study that indicates people who laugh live longer. Humor is a tension dissolver. It's an antidote to anxiety. It's a tranquilizer without any troublesome side effects. Laughter is life's shock absorber.

Someone once asked President Lincoln how he handled all the stresses of the Civil War. He said, "If it hadn't been for laughter, I could not have made it." Many famous comedians grew up in poor neighborhoods with lots of problems. They coped with their troubles by learning to laugh and make others laugh.

So learn to laugh. If you can laugh at it, you can live with it. And besides, if you learn to laugh at your troubles, you'll never run out of anything to laugh at!

One of my favorite verses in the Bible is Psalm 2:4: "The One enthroned in heaven laughs." Isn't that a great verse? God has a sense of humor. Have you ever seen the face of an orangutan? God thought that one up! Do you want to be more like God? Learn to laugh. A sense of humor can preserve your sanity.

God's timing is as marvelous as His sense of humor. As I was typing the notes for this chapter, my IBM Selectric typewriter totally ate up my outline. So I said to myself, "Self, you have a choice here. You can either practice what you preach and laugh this situation away, or you can get upset and irritated." I'm sure my wife and my kids were wondering what I was laughing about. Learn to laugh. It's relaxing.

Life is full of funny situations. Will Rogers once said, "I don't know any jokes. I just watch the government and report the facts." Proverbs 17:22 says, "Being cheerful keeps you healthy" (GNB). We all need to develop a sense of humor.

Deepen Your Love

The third step in becoming a patient person is to deepen your love. First Corinthians 13:4 is probably one of the most straightforward verses in the Bible: "Love is patient." Do you know what that means? It means that when I'm impatient, I'm being unloving because love is patient. When you love someone, you care about his needs, his desires, his hurts, his point of view, not just your own. When you are filled with love, almost nothing can provoke you to anger or cause you to be impatient. When you are filled with anger almost anything can provoke you. When you are under pressure, whatever is inside is going to come out. So deepen your love.

Ephesians 4:2 says, "Be patient with each other, making allowance for each other's faults because of your love" (TLB). Why should you be patient with others? "Because of your love."

There was one fellow in college who bugged me a lot. To make matters worse, he went out of his way to be around me. He was one of those people who kind of spit on you when he talked. It got so bad that when he'd walk down the hall at college, I would turn around and leave the building just to avoid him. I really did not like this guy; he was an irritation to me.

Then one night I read Ephesians 4:2 and it was like a dagger in my heart. "God, I don't love that guy." Remember a couple of chapters back I said you don't have to like them, but you do have to love them? Love is not a feeling; it's a choice. And it's an action. So I said, "God, help me to love this person tomorrow. Not forever. Just help me to love him tomorrow." And then I prayed a prayer that I later regretted. I said, "God, if this guy's irritating me is going to make me more like Christ, then make me like Christ. Teach me patience. If this guy's bugging me is going to make me more like You, I pray that tomorrow he'll irritate me more than I've ever been irritated before in my life." That was a mistake.

I got up the next morning and went to classes, but I didn't see him the whole day. I thought, "Hey, this is great. I love this way of learning patience. Right on, Lord." Then dinner time came. I walked into the cafeteria, got my meal, and sat down. As I'm eating my dinner, this guy spies me, saunters over, and says, "Hey, Rick, I haven't seen you all day!" He slams his plate down. His spaghetti covers my head and my shirt, and his Coke spills all over my pants. Everybody in the cafeteria turned to look at me, noodles dripping down my ears. But at that point I was filled with love and peace and joy because I was prepared. I really was. I had been praying all day, so I just said, "Praise the Lord." I'm sure everyone thought, "He's gone off his rocker."

What happens when you praise God for people who irritate you? You may become so much more like Jesus that they won't bother you anymore. Or, if it's the devil using that person to get at you, he'll stop because the situation is motivating you to praise God. If you learn to praise God in every situation, you'll develop a wall of praise around your life that even the devil cannot penetrate.

Depend on the Lord

The final step in developing patience is to depend on God. Patience is not merely a matter of human willpower; it's the fruit of the Spirit. You can't just psych yourself up and say, "I'm going to be patient if it kills me." It will. Patience is not willpower. Patience is not saying, "He doesn't really irritate me" when deep inside you're really thinking, *I hate that guy.* Patience is not wearing a mask and pretending.

If it's God's patience you feel, if it's the genuine fruit of the Spirit, you will have a genuine inner peace. Certain situations won't bother you the way they used to. Why? Because you are depending on the Lord.

Patience is a form of faith. It's saying, "I trust God. I believe that God is bigger than this problem. And I believe that God has His hand in these irritations and that He can use them in my life for good." Faith helps us look at life from God's point of view. Faith helps us say, "God, what do You want me to learn in this situation?" not, "Why did this happen?" Because of faith we no longer need to ask God, "Why did I get a flat tire while I was on the way to an important appointment?" Instead we can ask, "What do You want me to learn from this situation?"

Noah had to wait 120 years before it rained. That's a long time to be patient. Abraham waited 100 years to have a son. That's a long time to be patient. Moses waited 40 years in the wilderness and then spent another 40 years leading the Children of Israel across the wilderness to the Promised Land. That's a long time to be patient. Everyone in Old Testament times was waiting for the Messiah to come. In New Testament days, the disciples waited in the Upper Room for the Holy Spirit. The Bible is a book about waiting. Why? Because waiting demonstrates faith, and faith pleases God.

The hardest kind of waiting is waiting on God when you're in a hurry and He is not. It's hard to be patient when you're waiting for that answered prayer . . . when you're waiting for that miracle to happen . . . when you're waiting for God to change your financial condition, or your health problem, or your children, wife, husband, or that relative who is a kook. It's hard when you're in a hurry and God isn't, but waiting patiently is an evidence of faith. It's also a test of faith. How long can you wait?

Lazarus was a good friend of Jesus, but one day he got very sick. Mary and Martha, his sisters, sent word to Jesus saying, "Lord, the one You love is sick" (John 11:3). And the Bible says that when Jesus heard this, He purposely waited two more days before He set out for Bethany. By the time He arrived, Lazarus had died. His body was already sealed in the tomb.

Jesus arrived too late. Yet Jesus knew it wasn't too late. He walked up to the tomb and called, "Lazarus, come out" (John 11:43). Now you realize that He had to call Lazarus by name, because if He'd just said, "Come out," everyone in the world who was dead would have come out! So He had to be specific. "Lazarus, come out." And Lazarus did come out—alive!

What's the point? The point is this: God is never late. He is always on time. God's timing is perfect. He may not move on our schedule (He usually doesn't), but He is never late. He wants us to trust Him and wait on Him. The psalmist puts it this way: "Be still before the Lord and wait patiently for Him" (Ps. 37:7). Earlier in this psalm the writer has instructed us to *trust* in the Lord, to *delight* in Him, and to *commit* our way to Him. These are all aspects of faith and dependence. God longs for us to trust Him more than anything else. Patience is evidence of our faith in Him.

Why should we be patient? Because God is patient, and we are to be like Him. Peter urges us: "Bear in mind that our Lord's patience means salvation" (2 Peter 3:15). God is patient. If we are His children, we should bear the family likeness. That's why the Holy Spirit is at work in our lives, producing patience in us. It's a part of the character of Christ.

Chapter Seven

PUTTING ON 58
A LITTLE KINDNESS

In our study on the fruit of the Spirit, we've looked at love, joy, peace, and patience. Now we come to the fruit of kindness. Colossians 3:12 says, "Therefore, as God's chosen people, holy and dearly loved, clothe yourselves with compassion, kindness, humility, gentleness and patience." Notice the word *clothe*. The Greek word literally means "put on." What Paul is saying here is that when you wake up in the morning, you ought to get dressed spiritually and emotionally as well as physically. When you wake up in the morning and decide what to wear, you should also ask yourself, "What kind of attitude am I going to wear today?" Paul says kindness is a choice. It's something you can choose to "put on" every day.

Kindness is "love in action." Kindness is something you do. It's a practical expression of love. Kindness is something you can put your muscle into. It's visible and active, not just emotional. There's a song that says, "Find the need and fill it. Find the hurt and heal it." That's kindness.

Now, why should we be kind? After all, kindness can be risky. You might be misunderstood if you are kind to others. They might think, "Why is this person being so nice to us? What's in it for him?" People you are kind to also might take advantage of you. They might become a parasite, a leech, with the attitude: "Oh, here's a sucker. I'll milk him for all he's worth."

So why should we be kind? Two reasons. First, we should be kind because God is kind to us. Ephesians 2:8 in *The Living Bible* says, "Because of His kindness you have been saved through trusting Christ." Grace and kindness always go together. The poet Robert Burns said that the kind heart most resembles God. We should be kind just because God is kind to us.

The other reason we should be kind is because we want people to be kind to us. We want to be treated right. Jesus said, "Do to others what you would have them do to you" (Matt. 7:12). If you're rude to other people, they are going to be rude to you. But if you're kind, most people will want to respond the same way to you. Proverbs 21:21 says, "Be kind and honest and you will live a long life; others will respect you and treat you fairly" (GNB). And in Proverbs 11:17 we read, "Your own soul is nourished when you are kind; it is destroyed when you are cruel" (TLB). So when we're kind, we're really doing ourselves a favor.

How can we become more kind? What does it mean to be a kind person? Let me suggest five characteristics of a kind person.

Be Sensitive

First, a kind person is sensitive to others. He is aware of the needs of people around him. So become aware of the needs of those around you. Tune in to them. Kindness always starts with sensitivity. Philippians 2:4 says, "Each of you should look not only to your own interests, but also to the interests of others." Underline the word *look*. Kindness always starts with noticing the needs and hurts of others.

Often in marriage, we are totally unaware of what our partner's needs are. We have become calloused. We have stopped listening. We are oblivious to the pressure our mate is under. Simply stated, the root of many marriage problems is insensitivity.

Everyone you meet this week needs kindness because everyone is hurting somewhere. Even the people who sit around you at church have major hurts. You're just not aware of them most of the time. So kindness starts with sensitivity.

We find an example of sensitivity and kindness in the life of King David as recorded in 2 Samuel 9. David had been crowned king of Israel following Saul's death, and had led the Israelites in a series of military victories. His old enemy Saul, who had chased him for years, was dead. Saul's son Jonathan had also been killed. Now notice what David did. One of his actions as king was to ask if there was anyone left in Saul's family to whom he could be kind. He found a man who was Saul's grandson, Mephibosheth. How would you like to have that name—Mephibosheth? They probably called him "Phibi" for short. Besides having an unusual name, Mephibosheth was crippled in both feet.

When David sent for him, Mephibosheth probably thought, *I'm going to be killed because I'm part of the enemy family, the old dynasty.* But notice David's kind words: "Don't be afraid . . . for I will surely show you kindness for the sake of your father Jonathan. I will restore to you all the land that belonged to your grandfather Saul, and you will always eat at my table" (2 Sam. 9:7). Mephibosheth's response is interesting: "What is your servant, that you should notice a dead dog like me?" (v. 8) He apparently had a poor self-image. But the point is that David actively looked for people to whom he could be kind. He was sensitive. In your own life, whom do you need to be kind to this week? To whom do you need to be sensitive?

Be Supportive

A second characteristic exhibited by kind people is supportiveness. I'm talking about building people up rather than tearing them down. Watch what you say to people. Be supportive in your speech. Speak kindly. Proverbs 15:4 says, "Kind words bring life, but cruel words crush your spirit" (GNB). Do you like to be put down? Of course not. Nobody does. Children say, "Sticks and stones may break my bones, but names will never hurt me." Baloney! Names do hurt! Labels hurt! In fact, the Bible says that death and life are in the power of the tongue. You can destroy a person with what you say to him. So build people up with your words. Give everyone you meet an emotional lift. Encourage them. Be supportive.

Look at Proverbs 10:32: "Righteous people know the kind thing to say, but the wicked are always saying things that hurt" (GNB). Are you the kind of person who will pounce on a weakness in someone else? Maybe you do it in a joking manner, but you do it, and you enjoy doing it. Kind people don't embarrass others.

I saw a cartoon in which Charlie Brown is talking on the phone to a girl who says, "Hey, Chuck, guess what I'm running for? The Queen of the May at our school."

Charlie Brown says, "That's very interesting. Lucy has already been chosen at our school."

The girl on the phone responds, "Your school has pretty low standards, huh, Chuck?"

After Charlie Brown hangs up the phone, he looks at Lucy and says, "She says, 'Congratulations.' " Now that's diplomacy. That's kindness.

How supportive are you with your words? Do you encourage or do you discourage with your words? Do you lift up or tear down? Do you brag on your kids or do you nag them? Let me put it this way—if God gave you a dollar for every kind word you said and took away a dollar for every unkind word you said, would you be rich or poor? Learn to be sensitive. Be supportive in your speech.

Joseph is a good example of a man who spoke kind words. Everything seemed to go wrong in Joseph's life. His brothers treated him like dirt; they put him in a pit and sold him into slavery. Everything went wrong for thirty years of his life. But later the tables were turned, and Joseph became second in command in all of Egypt. His brothers came to him on bended knee, and at that time Joseph had the opportunity to retaliate and get even. But the Bible says that Joseph reassured them and spoke kindly to them, even after their father had died (Gen. 50:19-21). Kind words can rebuild a bridge in a strained relationship. A Christian ought to speak kindly even when given the opportunity to retaliate.

Be Sympathetic

A third characteristic of a kind person is the ability to be sympathetic. If you want to be kind, learn to be sympathetic. People appreciate it when you sympathize with them, when you feel with them and hurt with them. Many times when someone is experiencing a crisis, other people say, "We feel so awkward. We just don't know what to say at times like this." Well, you don't have to *say* anything. Just being there is an expression of kindness. Sometimes a touch on the shoulder, a tear, a pat on the back, or a grasp of the hand is all a hurting person needs. That's kindness. Romans 12:15 says: "When others are happy, be happy with them. If they are sad, share their sorrow" (TLB).

Regardless of what they think of his politics, most people admit that former President Reagan knew how to express heartfelt emotion. When the space shuttle exploded or when a plane carrying American soldiers crashed, he greeted the victims' families with a hug, a grasp of the hand, a tear in his eye. Strong leaders are not afraid to show emotion. Weak leaders, on the other hand, worry about what other people think. Strong leaders are strong enough to be sympathetic.

In 2 Timothy 2:24, Paul says that kindness is a mark of spiritual leadership. That means, men, that if you are not kind to your wife and children, you're not much of a spiritual leader, no matter how powerful or spiritual you appear in public. How long has it been since you helped with the dishes? How long has it been since you changed a diaper or helped pick up around the house? You say, "I'm the spiritual leader; I don't do that kind of thing." The Bible says kindness is a mark of a spiritual leader.

How do you respond when your teenager comes home with a broken heart? Do you say, "Oh, that's no big deal"? Or do you sympathize? Do you remember *your* teenage years—those years of self-conscious embarrassment? Do you remember when you got a pimple, and you felt like it was a national crisis? But now when your teenager mopes over a newly acquired zit, you say, "Oh, it's no big deal." Of course it's no big deal to you now, but remember that it was a big deal to you when you were a teenager and it's a big deal to your teenagers now. So sympathize with them.

Do you get excited about the things your kids get excited about? That's not childish, it's kindness. Get excited with those who are excited. Some people have to have a bomb explode under them before they'll get excited about anything. Rejoice with those who rejoice and weep with those who weep.

Now the supreme example of a sympathetic person is Jesus. In John 11:35 we read that Jesus wept at the tomb of Lazarus. (We looked at that incident briefly in chapter 6.) Jesus was not afraid to show emotion. He is called "the kindness and love of God" (Titus 3:4). Jesus is the embodiment of kindness. We often read in the Gospels that Jesus was "moved with compassion." If you want to know what kindness is like, just look at Jesus.

You must be kind if you want to be like Christ. No matter how many Scriptures you've memorized or how often you go to church, if you're not kind, you're not like Jesus. So learn to be a kind person by being sensitive, supportive, and sympathetic.

Be Straightforward

A kind person is also straightforward. Sometimes kindness means being candid. Sometimes it means laying it on the line, telling the truth, leveling with people. Sometimes the kindest thing you can do is be frank with a friend and tell him exactly where he is wrong. Proverbs 27:6 says, "Wounds from a friend are better than kisses from an enemy" (TLB). A real friend will level with you and say, "You're blowing it" or "You need to get in shape" or "You're messing up your life" or "You're making the biggest mistake of your life." A true friend will tell you these kinds of things.

Suppose a doctor examines you, and then he says either: "You must have surgery" or "Relax and don't worry about it." Which is the kinder statement? If you need surgery, the kind thing is for the doctor to tell you that you need it. Like a surgeon who takes his knife and cuts open a patient, we sometimes have to hurt people in order to heal them. Sometimes kindness means being straightforward.

We tend to sugarcoat kindness. The word brings to mind a picture of some little old lady with a white bun on her head. We don't realize that sometimes kindness means telling the painful truth. James Dobson has written a book entitled *Love Must Be Tough*. It's a great book. If you haven't read it, get it and read it. The book is about marriage and family relationships. Dobson explains that love sometimes means doing the tough thing, saying, "I'm not going to let you get away with this. I'm not going to sit by in silence and let you ruin our marriage." Sometimes I want to ask couples in counseling when they're going to care enough to get mad, when they'll say, "I want our marriage to work, and I'm not going to put up with this mess!" Loving husbands and wives care enough to confront. Likewise, out of kindness, parents sometimes have to confront their children and say, "No."

A biblical example of this kind of confrontation is found in

Galatians 2. Peter was visiting the church at Antioch, which was made up largely of Gentile Christians, and he was enjoying their fellowship. Peter had learned that as a Christian he didn't have to follow all the old Jewish customs. I think Peter probably developed a good taste for ham sandwiches: "Hey, these are good. I've been missing out all these years." When the Antioch Christians had picnics, Peter probably ate his ham sandwich and visited with his Gentile friends. But one day some Jewish Christians came down from Jerusalem to Antioch, and Peter said, "Well, maybe I had just better sit over here and pretend I'm not liberated." When Paul saw this, he said, "Peter, you're being a hypocrite." He said this because he cared. Paul cared for both Peter and the Gentile Christians, who were getting mixed messages. Paul cared enough to confront. Sometimes the kindest thing you can do is say, "You are messing up your life."

How do you know when to be confrontive? How do you know when to be tough rather than tender with people? Ask yourself two questions: First, am I really committed to this person's best interest? Second, am I making a "hit and run" comment, or do I plan to stick around to help my friend work on the change? Sometimes kindness means being straightforward—caring enough to confront—and saying, "I'm not going to let you destroy yourself. I'm not going to sit quietly and watch you mess up your life."

Be Spontaneous

Finally, if you want to be kind, learn to be spontaneous. Don't wait to show a kindness. Do it while you have the opportunity. Do it now. Be spontaneous.

Look at Galatians 6:10: "As we have opportunity, let us do good to all people, especially those who belong to the family of believers." Note the phrase *as we have opportunity.* When should we be kind? Whenever we have the opportunity.

Have you ever thought to yourself, *That person was really nice to me. I ought to write him a little thank-you note.* Or maybe you have thought, *I need to make that phone call,* or *I need to send a little gift,* or *I want to take something over to the neighbors?* Then you delay doing the kind deed. And you keep delaying until you are so embarrassed that you don't do it. Have you ever done that? I suppose we all have. When it comes to kindness though, good intentions don't count. The opportunity may not last until you "get around to it." Scripture says when you've got the opportunity to be kind, be spontaneous and do it.

When you get the slightest inclination to call your mother, do it. Write a note, share a prayer request, baby-sit, help around the house, wash the car, mow the lawn, whatever . . . just be kind whenever you have the opportunity.

The classic example of spontaneous kindness in Scripture is the good Samaritan. Remember the story? A man was hurt— beat up by robbers and left naked and half dead on the side of the road. A priest came along and looked at him and said, "Oh, I don't want to get near that guy. I'll be defiled." Another religious leader came along later and walked right on past. Then a Samaritan came by. (The Jews considered the Samaritans an inferior race.) This Samaritan bound up the man's wounds, took him to the nearest Holiday Inn, and left his American Express card with the innkeeper saying, "Take care of him and charge it to my account. I'll stop by on my way back."

Kindness costs, but when the Samaritan saw the need, he didn't think twice. He dropped everything. No hesitation. He was spontaneous. Contrast the Samaritan to the cold, calculating priest and the religious leader, who were trying to figure out if their contributions would be tax deductible. I'm sure the priest probably had plenty of excuses. Perhaps he thought, *Hey, I did my duty at the temple. I'm in a hurry to get home.* He might have thought, *If I stop and help that guy, I might get robbed myself. I've got to think of my family.* Maybe he thought, *It's not my fault he got hurt. He should have been more careful.* Or maybe he vowed to himself, "I'll campaign for better police protection on the road to Jericho."

Now here's the point: Jesus told this story to remind us of all the people who are hurting around us. They are hurting in their marriages. They are hurting at work. They are hurting physically. And they are hurting emotionally and spiritually. The question I must ask myself is: What is my excuse for not helping them? Why am I not a kind person?

If you don't get anything else out of this chapter, get this: *The number one enemy of kindness is busyness.* How often we say, "I'm just too busy. I don't have time to get involved. It might mess up my schedule. I have my priorities and pressures to think about. I'm too busy to fix a meal for my sick neighbor. I'm too busy to help with the preschoolers in Sunday School. I'm too busy. I don't have time." If that's your response, then you really are too busy, because the ministry of kindness is for everyone.

Be Kind to Someone This Week

Now let's narrow this down and be specific. It's one thing to read in a book about becoming a kind person, but it's another thing to consider how you are going to be kind this week. Take a few minutes to answer this question: How, specifically, can I be more kind this week? Kindness starts with sensitivity, so be aware. Open your eyes and look around you.

Your world is filled with people who need your kindness. How about at home? How can you be kind at home? I have seen so many struggling marriages that could be saved if people would just be kind to each other and treat each other with simple respect. One wife said, "The only time my husband talks to me is if he wants sex or wants me to change the channel on the TV." How can you be kind at home? You can start with common courtesy. Sometimes we are rudest to those closest to us. How about your kids? Are you kind to them? Do you pay close attention to them or do you just herd them here and there like cattle?

What about your crabby boss? You may not like the guy, but you can still be kind to him. How about that new coworker who doesn't know anything and is floundering at work because nobody has given him any orientation? How about that person who was unkind to you? Unkind people are the people who need the most kindness. They need massive doses of it.

Who can you be kind to at church? When you see a stranger, you can smile. You can sit next to a visitor. Welcome him. Shake his hand. Offer to give directions to a Sunday School class. When church members are kind to each other, they speak encouraging words to one another. They smile at people they don't know. Only a locked door could keep people out of a friendly church.

The point is this: There are as many ways to show kindness as there are people who need it. Let me suggest a project for you this week. Make a list of seven people to whom you can be kind. Also write down *how* you can show kindness to each one this week. Then ask God to give you the opportunity to show kindness to at least one of these people each day this week. You may be surprised how good this will make you feel. And you will probably find yourself exceeding your quota.

It's an interesting fact of history that the Romans confused the Greek word *christos* (Christ) with the word *chrestos,* which means "kind." See how many people you can *confuse* this week.

Chapter Eight

LIVING
THE GOOD LIFE

How would you define the word *good?* It's a word we use a lot. We talk about good food, good weather, and a good report. We say, "Have a good day"; "He did a good job"; "It's a good distance from here." The word is used in a lot of different ways.

When I was a teenager, my parents used to say, "Now have fun and be good." Your parents probably said that to you too. I always thought the statement was a contradiction. How could I have fun and be good at the same time?

I looked up the word *good* in Webster's dictionary and found seventeen different categories for the word with three or four different uses or illustrations under each category. Likewise, the Greek and Hebrew words for "good" and "goodness" used in the Bible are varied and full of meaning. The Bible has a lot to say about goodness. In fact, the words *good* or *goodness* are used 619 times in the Bible.

One of the phrases we hear a lot is "the good life." In my part of the country I hear, "Live the good life in Southern California!" But what is the good life?

What Is the Good Life?
For some people the good life means *looking good.* In America, looking good is serious business. Tanning salons, color coordination, hairdos, fat suction—whatever it takes—we've got to look good. We place a high premium on beauty and good looks. Do you know the problem with looking good? There is no universal standard. What looks good to you may not look good

to me. And what looks good to me may not look good to you. Have you ever fought with your kids about what clothes they should wear? Looking good means different things to different people.

Some people think the good life means *feeling good.* Whatever it takes they've got to feel good. That may mean sitting in a hot tub, going to Disneyland, or taking drugs. They pursue pleasure at all costs. Their standard of living has become "If it feels good, do it."

Some people think the good life means *having the goods.* They set about acquiring things, and if they get all the goodies, then they think they have a good life. It's like the bumper sticker I saw recently: "The one with the most toys at the end of life wins." For these people the whole object of life is to make money and spend it on goods.

The Bible presents a radically different picture of the good life. In His Word God says the good life is not based on looking good, feeling good, or having the goods. He says the good life is a life filled with goodness.

Now, what is goodness? Goodness is being and doing good. And when you are *being* good and *doing* good, you're going to feel good, and you're even going to start looking good—or at least looking better. But what *exactly* is goodness?

Genesis 1 records the creation of the universe, and reminds us that when God saw everything He created, He said it was good. Why? Because it fulfilled the purpose for which it was created. "Goodness" means fulfilling a purpose. It's being what God meant you to be.

God made you for a purpose. When you live the way God intended you to live, you will feel good. Your life will become meaningful. You will feel good because you're doing what God made you to do. Now what is that good thing for which God made you?

Ephesians 2:10 says, "For we are God's workmanship, *cre-*

ated in Christ Jesus *to do good works,* which God prepared in advance for us to do" (emphasis added). We're not saved *by* good works; we're saved *for* good works. The Christian lifestyle is to be a lifestyle of goodness. That is the main truth I want you to grasp from this chapter.

But why should you be good? How will you benefit from a lifestyle of goodness? The payoff is a healthy self-esteem. When you are doing good and being good, you will feel good about yourself because you're doing what God created you to do. This is a deeper sense of satisfaction than the satisfaction of self-centered pleasure-seekers. Lasting, healthy self-esteem doesn't come from looking good because looks fade. It doesn't come from feeling good because you won't feel good all the time, no matter what you do. And it doesn't come from having the goods because material possessions are often here today and gone tomorrow. Lasting self-esteem comes from doing good and being good. That's the purpose for which God made you.

We Aren't Naturally Good

But there's a problem—it's not our nature to be good. We were all born with a natural inclination toward selfishness. As I was flipping the channels on the TV recently, I heard a man saying, "My religion is the belief in the complete, inherent goodness of man." When I heard that, I just started laughing. Where had he been living for the past century—the North Pole? I don't buy the idea of man's inherent goodness at all. It doesn't make sense for four reasons.

First, the Bible says the inherent good of man is a fallacy. Isaiah 53:6 tells us that everyone wants to do his own thing, walk his own way, and be his own god. But nobody's perfect. Only God is naturally good (Mark 10:18). The rest of us have sinned and fall short of the glory of God (Rom. 3:23). So the Bible says man is not inherently good in all he does.

Second, we know that man cannot be inherently good because we have the facts of history. History is largely a record of man's inhumanity to man. Despite being the most educated and sophisticated generation ever, we still have wars, crime, violence, and prejudice. That's because the root of the problem is still present in us. We still selfishly seek our own way. History simply reflects the results of our actions.

The third reason I don't believe man is inherently good is because I'm a parent. If you're a parent, you know the idea that man is inherently good is a silly idea. I didn't have to teach my kids to lie. Did you? Of course not. It just comes naturally. I didn't have to teach my kids to be selfish. Did you? No. Man has an innate tendency to do wrong. The Bible says so, history proves it, and parents know it's so.

Reason number four to refute the goodness of man is the knowledge of my own heart. This may shock you, but the truth is that a lot of times I don't want to be good. In fact, a lot of times I like to sin! Sometimes I'd rather be unloving than loving; I'd rather return a smart remark than be patient. And sometimes I'm just plain selfish. I don't like to do what's good, even when I know it's the right thing to do. I want to be lazy instead. And even when my desire is right, even when I want to do good, I still struggle to actually do it.

Do you struggle to do good, even when you *want* to do what is right? God says this struggle is normal. "Can the Ethiopian change his skin or the leopard its spots? Neither can you do good who are accustomed to doing evil" (Jer. 13:23). He's saying it takes more than willpower to change your nature. You don't just snap your fingers and become a good person.

The Apostle Paul found that to be true in his own life. Perhaps you can identify with him. I can. In Romans 7, he says that no matter which way he turns, he can't make himself do right. He wants to, but he can't. When he wants to do good, he doesn't, and when he tries not to do wrong, he does it anyway. Can you identify with that? When we realize we're not perfect, we tend to comfort ourselves with comparisons: "Well, I may not be what I ought to be, but I'm better than so and so." You've probably heard someone say that. You may have even said it yourself. The only problem with this approach is that God doesn't grade on a curve. He doesn't judge us according to how good others are. Jesus Christ is His standard of measurement, and He is perfect. That means that when we measure ourselves by Christ, we don't measure up at all. We all fall short.

It's like the little boy who came to his mother and said, "Mommy, I'm eight feet tall."

She said, "You are?"

"Yes," he insisted. "I'm eight feet tall."

His mother asked what he measured himself with, and he pulled out a six-inch ruler.

We must evaluate ourselves by God's perfect standard of goodness, Jesus Christ. When we do that, we realize the truth that no one is perfectly good.

Our Goodness Is a Gift from God

God did not save us because of our goodness but because of His own kindness and mercy. Thanks to the saving work of Jesus Christ our Saviour, God can declare us good. Our goodness is a gift from God. We can't work for it. We can't earn it. We don't deserve it.

The Bible calls this *justification*. That's a big word that simply means God says you're OK because of what Jesus did for you. When you put your trust in Christ, God gives you a new nature. (It's like starting over; that's why it's called being "born again.") Then God not only gives you the desire to do good, but He also gives you the power to do good. Philippians 2:13 says, "It is God who works in you both *to will* and *to do* for His good pleasure" (NKJV, emphasis added). He gives you the *desire* and the *power* to do what is right. That's one of the ways you know you are a Christian.

By God's grace and power we are first re-created as good people, and then we are given the ability to do good deeds. God works from the inside out, not from the outside in. He says, "Let Me change you on the inside and the outside will fall into place." Now, what does that mean? Does it mean that a Christian never sins? Of course not. All of us make mistakes. All of us sin. What it means is now that I'm a Christian I have a new power and a new desire to do what's right. God solved the problem of my old selfish nature by giving me a new Christlike nature.

God has done the work of changing my nature. Now I need to cooperate with His efforts and work at letting His goodness fill me. Titus 3:14 says we must *learn* to do good. Here are five simple suggestions for learning to do good.

Master Your Bible
First, become a student of God's Word. Read the Bible, study it, and memorize it. Fill your mind and your life with it. You have only two sources from which to develop your values: the world or the Word. The choice is up to you.

I was once given a new Bible, and the person who gave it to me wrote in the front of it: *This book will keep you from sin, or sin will keep you from this book.* That's true. In 2 Timothy 3:16 Paul writes: "The whole Bible was given to us by inspiration from God and is useful to teach us what is true and to make us realize what is wrong in our lives; it straightens us out and helps us do what is right" (TLB). So, master the Bible if you want to do good. Fill your life with it.

It's not enough to own a Bible, you've got to use it. A Bible in the hand is worth two on the shelf. If I were to ask you if you believe the Bible from cover to cover, you would probably say you do. You believe the Bible from cover to cover, but have you read it from cover to cover? How do you know you believe it if you don't even know what's in it?

Some Christians are more faithful to Ann Landers than they are to God's Word. They are more faithful to the sports page. They wouldn't think of going to bed without reading the stock report. They devour the paper every day, but they go day after day after day without cracking open the Bible. And the Bible is what teaches us to know right from wrong.

Perhaps you are saying, "Well, Rick, I don't understand the Bible." The solution is simple. Get a modern version. There are many good ones. Get a *Good News Bible* or a *Living Bible*. Get a good study Bible like the *New International Version Study Bible* or *The Life Application Bible*. When someone says, "I don't understand the Bible," I'm reminded of Mark Twain, who said, "It's not the parts of the Bible that I don't understand that bother me, it's the part that I do understand." Don't you find that to be true?

When I see a person whose Bible is falling apart, I've discovered that the person usually isn't. Master the Bible.

Guard Your Mind
Second, if you want to do good, you must learn to control your thought life. I realize I've said this repeatedly in this book, but it's essential because as a man thinks in his heart, so is he. Sin always starts in the mind. Satan plants ideas, called temptations, in your head. If you nurture these temptations in your mind, they will become visible in your life. Sin always starts in your mind, so guard your mind.

Most people are very careless about what they allow to enter their minds. I'm amazed at what some Christians watch on TV. They say, "Oh, it doesn't bother me to watch that kind of stuff." Baloney! Look at what Jesus says in Matthew 6:22: "The eye is the lamp of the body. If your eyes are good, your whole body will be full of light." The next verse, in *The Living*

Bible, says, "But if your eye is clouded with evil thoughts and desires, you are in deep spiritual darkness." Psychiatrists, psychologists, and other experts now say that you never really forget anything. You may not remember it all consciously, but everything you've seen or heard is in your subconscious. It all gets mixed up in your mind, and that's why you have those crazy dreams. So guard your mind. Be discriminating. Don't just let anything come into your mind.

When you are bombarded with garbage on the television, you have a choice. You can change the channel or, better yet, you can turn the set off and spend some time in God's Word. If you want to do good, think about good, positive, and uplifting things—things that are true, honest, pure, and of good report (Phil. 4:8, KJV). Stop allowing poisonous material to enter your mind. If you want to do good, you've got to be more careful with what you give your attention to. Guard your mind.

Develop Convictions
Third, if you want to learn to do good, you must develop some convictions. What do you stand for? It's been said that if you don't stand for something, you'll fall for anything. This is especially true in America's pluralistic society where tolerance for opposing viewpoints is a prized virtue. We love to appear open-minded. The problem is some people are so open-minded that their brains fall out! They don't stand for anything.

Do you know the difference between an opinion and a conviction? An opinion is something that you hold; a conviction is something that holds you. An opinion is something you'll argue about. A conviction is something you will suffer for and, if necessary, die for.

Did you realize that Christians are supposed to hate some things? Romans 12:9 says, "Hate what is evil; cling to what is good." That's pretty clear. We are supposed to hate evil. Why? One of the reasons is because of what evil does to people. Evil hurts people. It destroys people. When you take a close look at Jesus, you realize that goodness means standing for what is right and standing against what is wrong. He hated sin but loved sinners. We tend to do the exact opposite. We hate sinners and love sin. But God wants us to have both compassion for people and conviction against sin.

Goodness demands some gutsy conviction—taking a stand against things like child abuse, abortion, pornography, and corruption. I heard on the radio recently that one out of every four little girls in America will be molested by the time she is 18. We've got to take a stand against evil like that! Christians also need to speak up when someone takes the Lord's name in vain. Have some conviction. When you hear about some dishonest activity, speak out against it. Edmund Burke once said, "All that is necessary for evil to triumph is for good men to do nothing." Develop some convictions.

You need to realize, of course, that if you develop some convictions, you won't be popular with everyone. Some people will call you a fanatic or a religious nut. When that happens, remember that Peter says it's better to suffer for doing good than for doing evil (1 Peter 2:19-20). Jesus warned us that the more we identify with Him, the more the world around us will respond with hostility.

If you stand up for your convictions, you can count on opposition. Some people will disagree with you. The Bible says that in the last days there will be people who hate good (2 Tim. 3:3). Remember that Jesus Christ lived a perfect life, yet He was criticized, mocked, misunderstood, and eventually killed on a cross. So what makes you think life will be any easier for you—or me? That leads me to the fourth step.

Muster the Courage to Be Different

If you are going to learn to do good, you must have the courage to be different from your culture. Now that's scary because our society puts all of these pressures on us to conform, to go with the flow. You have to "go along to get along." When you go to the office party, you're expected to act the way others do. We're all encouraged to act alike, talk alike, dress alike, and smell alike just to fit in. But sometimes goodness means being willing to stand alone. Dare to be different. As 3 John 11 says, "Do not imitate what is evil but what is good."

Do you remember the story of the three young Israelite men who wouldn't bow down to the statue of King Nebuchadnezzar and were thrown into the fiery furnace? When you are a person of integrity, you're going to go through the fire. You can count on it.

Speaking of heat, let me ask you, are you a thermostat or a thermometer? You're either one or the other. What does a thermometer do? It registers the temperature. It simply reflects its environment, whether it's hot or cold. A thermostat, on the other hand, *controls* the temperature. It influences its environment. It sets the standard. Which are you, a thermometer or a thermostat?

One of my favorite verses in the Bible is 1 Peter 3:13. The author writes of having a "passion for goodness" (MOFFATT). Goodness means more than just avoiding evil. Goodness also means being enthusiastic for what's right. We should promote what's positive and good.

In Romans 15, Paul compliments the Christians in Rome. He says, "You . . . are full of goodness" (v. 14). Now at that time Rome was the sin capital of the ancient world. It would make Las Vegas look like a Sunday School picnic. Every kind of debauchery and immorality you could think of was going on in Rome. And when in Rome, what are you expected to do? You are expected to do as the Romans do! But a certain band of people refused to indulge in such sinful behavior. They had integrity. And Paul writes to them and says, "In the middle of this cesspool, you are full of goodness." What a testimony! What a reputation! Wouldn't you like to have that kind of reputation?

Meet with Other Believers

Finally, if you want to do good, you must develop the habit of meeting with other believers. One secret of the Roman Christians' goodness was that they were good together. They met together regularly to challenge and encourage and support one another in their Christian lifestyle. The author of Hebrews tells us to "consider how we may spur one another on toward love and good deeds." Then he adds this important ingredient: "Let us not give up meeting together . . . but let us encourage one another" (Heb. 10:24-25).

Our fellowship with other believers is designed to encourage us to live good lives in an evil world. As Christians we are not to imitate the world, but neither are we to live in isolation from it. Both extreme approaches to the world are wrong. Rather, we are to learn to live *in* the world without being *of* the world. That was Jesus' prayer for His followers in John 17. He also prayed, "My prayer is not that You take them out of the world but that you protect them from the evil one" (v. 15). The answer is not imitation or isolation, but *insulation*. God *will* protect us from evil, and one of the most powerful means He uses to do that is the church.

You don't find soldiers going out on their own to do battle with the enemy forces. They go in groups called companies or platoons or battalions. They know they need each other. Why, then, do so many Christians think they can go it alone in life? Don't they realize they are in a battle with spiritual forces of evil? (Eph. 6) Don't they recognize the dangers? I honestly think many Christians don't even know there's a war going on. They're so out of touch with spiritual realities they really don't recognize they're in the middle of a battle.

But Christians who know the score realize they need each other. They enjoy church gatherings as *R & R* from the front lines of battle. They see the worship service as a spiritual service station, where they can get filled up and tuned up and prepared to go back to the battle.

The Christian life is not easy, but it is eternally worthwhile. And doing good isn't always easy, but there is a reward. Galatians 6:9 says, "Let us not become weary in doing good, for at the proper time we will reap a harvest if we do not give up." How do you fight the weariness? How do you keep on keeping on? By mastering the Bible, by guarding your mind, by developing some convictions, by having the courage to be different, and by meeting regularly with other Christians for support and encouragement.

What about you? Are you satisfied to be a thermometer, simply registering the spiritual coldness of the environment around you. Or are you willing to be God's thermostat in your corner of the world? Use your influence for God and for good in your world this week! P305

Chapter Nine

68

THE ONE WHO CAN BE COUNTED ON

So far in our study of the fruit of the Spirit, we've looked at love, joy, peace, patience, kindness, and goodness. In this chapter, we will consider the quality of faithfulness. You may be saying to yourself, "I'm not sure I can take on any more. I haven't mastered patience, yet." Don't despair. Remember, it's the *fruit* of the Spirit—singular. All nine qualities are inter-related and grow together.

Faithfulness. Can you be counted on? Faithfulness is not a word we hear very often these days. It's usually a word reserved for retirement parties. After 25 years of faithful service, you get a gold watch. When most of us think of the word *faithful*, we think of things that are old. My dog may be old and ugly, but he's faithful. My car may be old and ugly, but it's faithful.

But what does it mean to be faithful? It means to be reliable. It means to be trustworthy, dependable, consistent. Faithfulness is a rare quality. The Bible says, "Who can find a faithful man?" (Prov. 20:6, NKJV) It's not easy to find someone who can *really* be counted on. The *Good News Bible* translates Proverbs 20:6 this way: "Everyone talks about how loyal and faithful he is, but just try to find someone who really is!" As a pastor, I've learned that not everyone who volunteers to serve actually comes through.

Why is faithfulness so important in the Christian life? In the first place, we should be faithful because God is faithful. Psalm 33:4 says, "He is faithful in all He does." Since God desires for us to be like Him, He wants us to learn to be faithful.

In addition, faithfulness makes life so much easier. Unfaithfulness is the cause of so many problems in life. Proverbs 25:19 says, "Like a bad tooth or a lame foot is reliance on the unfaithful in times of trouble." Do you know what the writer is saying? He's saying that unreliable people are a pain—like a bad toothache. They're like a limp foot. You know what it's like to have a bunion or a corn on your foot. It hurts. When you're depending on an unreliable person, you can never quite relax. In the back of your mind you're always wondering, "Will he let me down again or will he come through this time?" Working with inconsistent people is extremely frustrating.

We all look for faithfulness in others as we go about our daily activities. We want the paper boy to be reliable. We want the postman to be faithful. When I mail a letter, I depend on the mail service to get it there. I want the food at my favorite restaurant to be consistent from week to week.

The most famous geyser in America is Old Faithful at Yellowstone National Park. Old Faithful is not the biggest geyser in America. And it's not the most powerful geyser in America. What makes it famous is its faithfulness! It's like clockwork. Dependable. People appreciate dependability, even in a geyser.

Let me ask you, who can count on you? Do you have a reputation for being reliable? Would someone who knows you well stake his life on your faithfulness? Few things are more important than faithfulness. You may be talented, educated, and creative but if you're not dependable, your talents aren't worth much. Someone has said, "The greatest ability is dependability."

Another reason why we should be faithful is that God rewards faithfulness. In the Parable of the Talents recorded in Matthew 25, Jesus says that one day God is going to judge us. But this judgment will not evaluate our ability or good intentions. God is going to judge us and reward us according to our faithfulness. The Bible says a faithful man will be richly blessed. So if you want to be rewarded in heaven, you should learn how to become a faithful, dependable person.

God wants us to be faithful *in* our relationships and *with* our resources. Let me suggest eight characteristics of faithfulness. I'll express these as imperatives—things you need to do in order to develop the quality of faithfulness in your life.

Keep Your Promises

Proverbs 25:14 says, "Like clouds and wind without rain is a man who boasts of gifts he does not give." Do you know people like that? They make promises but never keep them. They may say, "I'm aiming to do it," but they never get around to it.

Be careful about the promises you make. Have you ever told someone you'd call them back later and then didn't do it? Have you ever said, "The check is in the mail" before it was? Have you ever promised you'd pray for someone and then forgotten to? You need to be dependable when you say, "I'll return it soon," or "We'll do it later." Keep your word!

Sometimes as a parent, in a moment of weakness, I make promises to my kids just to get them out of my hair. Do you ever do that? I promise them something that doesn't even register in my mind. Weeks later I may not remember what I said, but I've learned that my kids never forget anything. Never. When I say, "Well, we might, *maybe*, do something," they interpret my words to mean we are *definitely* doing something. Start packing. You've got to keep your promises.

Proverbs 20:25 says, "It is a trap for a man to dedicate something rashly and only later to consider his vows." In other words, it's always easier to get in than it is to get out. Do you know the number one problem in parent/child relationships? Resentment. And the number one cause of resentment is broken promises.

Ecclesiastes 5:5 says, "It is better not to vow than to make a vow and not fulfill it." Husbands, what promises do you need to keep? Have you promised to take your wife on a vacation, or have you promised to repair a leaky faucet or help with a special project? What about your kids? Have you promised to spend more time together or play baseball?

When you are dependable, you don't have to convince people that you are. You don't have to make a big deal of it. You don't have to say "cross my heart, hope to die, stick a needle in my eye." No, you just say you'll do it and then you do it! Jesus said to let your yes be yes and your no be no (Matt. 5:37). Over time, your track record will speak for itself. Others will feel confident that they can count on you. And God will be making careful notes in heaven.

Honor Your Marriage

In a wedding ceremony the bride and groom exchange rings as a symbol of the vow they are making. They promise to be faithful to each other for the rest of their lives. Faithfulness. You don't have to commit adultery to be unfaithful. All you have to do is let something else take priority over your marriage. This can be anything . . . sports, community activities, television, or work. Some people have a love affair with their work. But the Bible says if you are married, your relationship to your mate is to be second only to your relationship to God. Hebrews 13:4 says: "Marriage should be honored by all." Circle that word *honored*. The word means "to hold in respect," "to value with high esteem," and "to take seriously."

If you want to develop the quality of faithfulness, honor your marriage. Put effort into it. The love chapter, 1 Corinthians 13, says when you love someone the one you love can count on you. What does that mean? It means being loving and being dependable go hand in hand. The flip side of that means that when I am unreliable, I'm not loving. Faithfulness is a choice.

It's not dependent on what others do. You make a commitment, and regardless of what your mate does, you choose to be faithful to the vows you made before God. Keep your promises and honor your marriage.

Use Your Talents
In 1 Peter 4:10 we read, "Each one should use whatever gift he has received to serve others, faithfully administering God's grace in its various forms." Now the fact is that God has given you some spiritual abilities, some talents, some gifts. He has made an investment in you, and He wants and expects a return on that investment. If you don't use the talents you have been given, other people will be cheated because you aren't contributing what God has uniquely equipped you to provide.

If you want to become more faithful, use your talents. You might say, "Well, I'm not talented like so and so. I can't sing like she can." Just because you can't do the spectacular, you are not excused from doing what you can. Faithfulness does not depend on what I *don't* have or *can't* do. Faithfulness depends on what I do with what I have. I'm not responsible to sing to God if He didn't give me that gift. But I am responsible to use the gifts and talents God has given me.

We can't all be brilliant, but we can all be faithful. And faithfulness is what counts with God! So keep your promises, honor your marriage, and use your talents.

Make the Most of Your Time
Time is something we all have in common. Everyone has the same amount of time—168 hours a week. Ephesians 5:15 says, "Live life, then, with a due sense of responsibility, not as men who do not know the meaning of life but as those who do. Make the best use of your time" (PH).

There are three things you can do with your time. You can spend it, you can waste it, or you can invest it. The best use of your time is to invest it in something that is going to outlast you. Faithfulness involves time management.

There are two primary time wasters: regret and worry. When we regret the past, we waste huge amounts of time looking backward to change something we can't change anyway. When we worry about the future, we waste time fretting over events that may never happen. As a result, we waste the time and energy allotted for today. In order to become a more faithful person, you're going to have to give up what I call *When and Then Thinking.* "*When* the kids start school . . . *when* the kids finish school . . . *when* the grandkids start school . . . *when* I retire . . . *when* we pay all the bills, *then* I'll be able to serve the Lord." God says be faithful now.

Let me offer you a guilt-relieving statement: God understands your schedule. He really does. He understands it better than you do. So what should you do? Talk to Him about it. Say, "God, tell me what I need to cut out. Tell me what I need to add." When you burn the candle at both ends, you're not as bright as you think you are. You probably need to cut out some things. And you may need to add some other things. God can help you make these choices.

So make your time count. It's a part of being faithful.

Stand by Your Friends

Another way to develop your faithfulness is to cultivate personal loyalty. A faithful person stands by his or her friends. Proverbs 17:17 says, "A true friend is always loyal, and a brother is born to help in time of need" (TLB). Genuine friends are consistent. They are reliable. They can be counted on in a crisis. Someone has said that when times get tough, a genuine friend doesn't see through you but sees you through. To whom are you loyal? Who can count on you? Do they know it?

A few years ago the associate pastor in the church I serve took me out to lunch, and as we sat down, he said, "I just want to say one thing. No matter what happens, I'll always be your friend." Loyalty like that is a priceless treasure. You can't put a price tag on it.

If I asked you to write letters to five people you knew you could count on, to whom would you write? What if I turned it around? Who would write to you and say, "I know I can depend on you if things get tough"? Stand by your friends.

Manage Your Money
If you want to develop the fruit of faithfulness, you must learn to manage your money. God has given you resources, and the Bible says how you handle money is a test of your faithfulness to Him. Jesus said, "If you have not been trustworthy in handling worldly wealth, who will trust you with true riches?" (Luke 16:11). Amazing! God says that if you're not faithful with your material possessions, He will not trust you with spiritual resources! So you need to ask yourself questions like, "Am I faithful in tithing to the Lord? Do I pay my bills on time? When I compare my giving to my spending and my spending to my savings, is my life really in balance? Am I being a wise manager of the money God has given me?" The truth is that the way you handle your finances determines to a large extent what God can do in your life. That's what God says! If God can't trust you with earthly wealth, He won't trust you with spiritual wealth.

Now what does it mean to be faithful with your finances? Specifically, what does it mean to be faithful in giving? First Corinthians 16:2 says, "On every Lord's Day each of you should put aside something from what you have earned during the week, and use it for this offering. The amount depends on how much the Lord has helped you earn" (TLB). That verse defines what it means to be a faithful giver. It says three things.

First, we should give **regularly.** We are to give weekly, on every Sunday. A faithful person's giving is systematic, not spasmodic. It's not, "Oh, I feel good today. I'm going to tip God. Here, Lord." I used to think that the most spiritual giving occurred when a person was impulsively moved by emotion to give. Not true. God says giving should be consistent, *every* Sunday, whether we feel like it or not. This principle relates to the second aspect of faithful giving.

God says your giving should be planned. You should prayerfully plan and set aside something from what you've earned. If you're married, you should sit down with your mate and discuss the amount you feel God wants you to give each week. If you don't plan it, you won't give consistently. Remember, God is looking for faithfulness.

My wife and I have a tithe account. We've found that the only way we can be faithful in our giving is to keep a record of it. So we actually have a tithe account in our ledger. It's account Number One. Before we pay any bills, we return our tithe to the Lord. The ledger helps us to be faithful.

Finally, faithful giving is proportional; it's a percentage of your income. The amount you should give depends on how much the Lord has helped you earn. That's what tithing is all about. A tithe means 10 percent. Giving 10 percent should be the minimum—the starting point. If God has richly blessed you financially, you may be able to give much more than 10 percent. We are to give back to God a percentage of what He enables us to earn.

So keep your promises, honor your marriage, use your talents, make the most of your time, stand by your friends, and manage your money. These are practical ways to become more faithful.

Do Your Best at Work
If you were responsible for hiring people at work, what would you look for? I would guess one of the things you'd look for is

dependability. Since I became a pastor, I think I've filled out a reference form on someone practically every week. And I've never seen a reference form that doesn't mention dependability, trustworthiness, punctuality, reliability, or consistency. Employers, colleges, and mission agencies all want to know about a person's faithfulness in work habits.

How can your work affect your faithfulness? Jesus says, "Whoever can be trusted with very little can also be trusted with much" (Luke 16:10). So your faithfulness is affected by how you handle the little things of life. You see, life is largely made up of little things, so if you're not faithful in the little things, you won't be faithful in most of life. The same thing is true of spiritual growth. The little things, like having a daily quiet time and prayer, produce big results. Success comes from being faithful in the little things that other people overlook.

Do you have a guilt pile at work? Most people do. It's that little pile of things you haven't gotten around to yet. Faithfulness includes how you handle your guilt pile. It may not mean much to you that someone has written you a letter, but the writer of that letter expects an answer. His world may be depending on it. How do you handle the little things in life?

Faithfulness is also affected by how we handle what's not ours. Jesus said, "And if you have not been trustworthy with someone else's property, who will give you property of your own?" (Luke 16:12) When I'm at work, am I as trustworthy with the supplies as if I were paying for them? If I ran a business, would I be taking extra coffee breaks? If I rent a rototiller to use on my lawn, do I take as good care of it as I would one I owned? Would I want to buy the rental car I just abused for a week? How do you handle things that aren't yours? God says that's a test of faithfulness.

See how practical this is? Faithfulness is important in so many different areas of our lives. That's why God says you're going to be rewarded for your faithfulness. Do your best at work. The Bible says, "Whatever you do, work at it with all your heart, as working for the Lord, not for men" (Col. 3:23). Christians ought to have a reputation for being the most dependable people at work. They are always aware of who their true boss is!

Commit Yourself to a Church

An eighth way you can develop faithfulness is to commit yourself to a specific, local body of believers. Romans 12:5 says, "So in Christ we who are many form one body, and each member belongs to all the others." Each believer belongs to all the others in the body of Christ. This is why the local church is so important.

The Bible says Christians are engaged in a spiritual battle (Eph. 6:10-18). The words used in the Bible to describe the Christian life are war terms: *fight, conquer, strive, battle, overcome, victory.* And Christians are likened to soldiers (2 Tim. 2:3). The Apostle Paul tells us to "put on the full armor of God" (Eph. 6:11). You're in a spiritual battle whether you know it or not, and you need support and reinforcement. When you became a Christian, you signed up to be part of God's army.

Now suppose I go to a recruiting office and say I want to join the army. They say, "Great, sign here on the dotted line." Then I say, "Well, wait a minute. I want to join the army, but I have one condition. I don't want to be committed to any specific platoon. I want to be able to float around from platoon to platoon. I'll be a part of the army, but I don't want to be committed to a specific group of soldiers. If the battle gets a little hot in one area, I'll move to another area and join another platoon. And if I don't like one platoon's leadership, I'll join another platoon." Would you like to have someone like that fighting by your side in a foxhole? Of course not! Yet that is how many Christians today relate to God's army. They float around from church to church with little or no commitment to any specific group of Christians. So while the battle is being fought, they're AWOL.

When you became a Christian, you committed yourself to Jesus Christ. Now you can become a part of the local body of believers by committing yourself to those people. That's what "church membership" is—a commitment to other Christians. It's a decision to become a participant, not merely a spectator. You stop being a consumer and become a contributor.

Having traveled many places overseas, I've discovered that "free-floating" believers are a phenomena found only in America. Nowhere else in the world will you find people who claim to be believers but are not committed to any local fellowship.

I like what my wife said when someone asked her what the difference was between just attending a church and becoming a member of one. She said, "It's like the difference between getting married and just living together. The difference is commitment."

Who can count on you? Can anyone count on you? There is no such thing as a Lone Ranger Christian. *Koinonia*, the Greek word used in the Bible to mean "fellowship," means being as committed to each other as we are to Jesus Christ. Jesus said, "By this all men will know that you are My disciples, if you love one another" (John 13:35). One way love expresses itself is in faithfulness to others.

Whether it's keeping your promises, honoring your marriage, being committed to your church, doing your best at work, or being loyal to your friends, God will honor your faithfulness. Why? Because He wants us to become more and more like Jesus Christ, who was faithful unto death.

You cannot overestimate the importance of faithfulness. Jesus told the parable of the master who went away and left his servants in charge. When he returned, the servants were rewarded not for their ability, or their knowledge, or their good intentions, but for their faithfulness. Jesus has left you and me in charge of His business here on earth, and one day He is coming back. When He returns, will He find us faithful?

Chapter Ten

A
GENTLE APPROACH

Everyone wants friends. Everyone needs friends. It's a medical fact that you live longer if you have friends. Dr. James Lynch has done extensive research that proves that loneliness actually weakens a person's immune system.

Years ago, Dale Carnegie wrote the number two best-selling book of this century entitled *How to Win Friends and Influence People.* Why has it sold so many copies? Because everyone wants to be liked by others. We all want friends. A verse in Proverbs states: "A man who wants to have friends must show himself friendly" (18:24, KJV). In other words, if you want to be liked by others, it helps if you are likable. And one of the most likable qualities is what the Bible calls "gentleness."

In the 1980s many people went to the movies and enjoyed watching tough characters like Dirty Harry and Rambo, but nobody really wants to live with those kinds of people. We want people around us to be understanding, kind, and gentle. What is gentleness? Based on the original Greek word used in the New Testament, the word gentleness literally means "strength under control." The word was used to describe a wild stallion that had been tamed or broken. The tamed stallion still had as much power and energy as when it was wild, but it could now be controlled and made useful for its master. To be gentle doesn't mean to be weak, to be a wimp. Interestingly, only two people in the Bible were called gentle—Jesus and Moses—and neither of them were weak men. Both were very strong, masculine men.

Galatians 5:23 says the eighth fruit of the Spirit is gentleness. And Philippians 4:5 tells us to "show a gentle attitude toward everyone" (GNB). Now what does it mean to be gentle? It means controlling your reactions to people. It means *choosing* your own response to people rather than simply reacting to them.

In this chapter we'll consider six types of people with whom you can practice gentleness. They are people you come in contact with all the time.

Be Understanding, Not Demanding

When someone *serves* you, *be understanding, not demanding.* Philippians 2:4-5 says, "Don't just think about your own affairs, but be interested in others, too, and in what they are doing" (TLB).

Now let me ask you, how do you treat people who provide a service to you? How do you treat the waitresses, clerks, secretaries, employees, bank tellers, and others who serve you? Are you rude and demanding? Or are you indifferent and impersonal as if they were just part of the machinery? Do you understand that they may have had a hard day too, or do you only think of yourself? The first way you can develop gentleness is to work at understanding the people who serve you.

I have learned the secret of getting great service in a restaurant. Here it is: treat those who serve you with respect. It's amazing how much more helpful waiters and waitresses are when you're considerate of their feelings and when you are sympathetic to the pressure they are under. Looking beyond your own needs and agenda takes a little effort, but the results are well worth the effort.

I read a popular self-help book once in which the author stated that when you must return defective merchandise, you should ignore the clerk and complain directly to the head man. While this approach may be effective, the author showed no respect for clerks by boldly proclaiming, "All clerks are jerks." That's being demanding instead of understanding.

The first place you can be gentle is at home. The Bible says that wives are to adorn themselves with "a gentle and quiet spirit" (1 Peter 3:4). That's more valuable than any clothes you can wear or any perfume you can put on. Gentleness is an attractive attribute for a woman.

The Bible says to husbands: "You husbands should try to understand the wives you live with" (1 Peter 3:7, PH). Be understanding, not demanding toward people who serve you, and toward the people with whom you live.

Be Gracious, Not Judgmental

When someone *disappoints* you, *be gracious, not judgmental.* Galatians 6:1-2 says, "If someone is caught in a sin, you who are spiritual should restore him gently. But watch yourself, or you also may be tempted." The temptation Paul is referring to in this passage may well be the temptation to be judgmental, to be "holier than thou." And that's the wrong response for a Christian to have toward a brother or sister in Christ who is struggling with sin. Romans 14:1 says, "Accept him whose faith is weak, without passing judgment on disputable matters." We set ourselves up for Satan's attack in our own areas of weakness the moment we begin to judge others.

Let me ask you, what's your reaction to people when they mess up their lives? Do you secretly think, *I told you so,* or *I could see it coming,* or *It serves you right,* or *How could you be so dumb?* Does it give you an inward sense of superiority? Jesus' reaction to the woman caught committing adultery was full of sensitivity. He defended her in front of other people and then, after the crowd had left, He dealt with her privately about her sin. He was gracious, not judgmental.

Why should we work at not being judgmental? Because that's the way Christ has treated us. Romans 15:7 says, "Accept one another, then, just as Christ accepted you, in order to bring praise to God." You know, God puts up with a lot from us. And if God puts up with our inconsistencies and weaknesses, we can learn to put up with other's shortcomings. Whenever you feel tempted to judge another person, pause to remember how much God has forgiven you. The more you recognize God's grace to you, the more gracious you will be to others.

You will become more gentle when you are understanding, not demanding of the people who serve you. And when people disappoint you, you will become more gentle when you learn to act graciously toward them and not judge them. You don't rub it in, you rub it out! God is consistently gentle with you. And He wants you to be gentle with others.

Be Tender without Surrender

When someone *disagrees* with you, *be tender without surrender*. It's a fact of life that you'll never be able to please everyone. You will always meet people who like to argue and quarrel with you. Some people will contradict everything you say. How should you respond to these people?

One of the tests of spiritual maturity is how you handle people who disagree with you. Some people have a need to devastate everyone who disagrees with them. If you challenge them or offer a comparison, complaint, or criticism, they respond with a full-blown personal attack. Then what do you do? You have three alternatives: you can retreat in fear, you can react in anger, or you can respond in gentleness. Most people choose between retreating or reacting. Few know how to respond in gentleness.

If you give in and retreat in fear from argumentative people, you say, "OK, have it your way." "Peace at any price" brings many hidden costs to any relationship.

On the other hand, if you react in anger, you take the

offensive and fight back every time someone opposes you. Anger is usually a telltale sign that you feel insecure and threatened by someone's disapproval. And anger is a warning light that tells you you are about to lose something, often your self-esteem. When people become angry, the most common reaction is to become sarcastic and attack the other person's self-worth.

The third alternative, responding in gentleness, is the approach God wants you to take to opposition. This kind of response requires a fine balance between maintaining your right to an opinion while equally respecting another's right to his or her opinion. It requires being tender without surrendering your convictions.

Proverbs 15:1 says, "A gentle answer quiets anger, but a harsh one stirs it up" (GNB). I'm sure you've found that to be true in your experience. I have. When someone asks you a question, if you respond arrogantly, the questioner will probably challenge you. But if you respond quietly, the questioner is more likely to be open to your answer. When you shout at people in a loud voice, they get very defensive.

James 3:16-17 says, "Where there is jealousy and selfishness, there is also disorder and every kind of evil. But the wisdom from above is pure first of all; it is also *peaceful, gentle, and friendly*" (GNB). James pinpoints the cause of quarrels and arguments: selfishness—wanting our own way and demanding that others agree with us. But he goes on to say that if you are a wise person, you are peaceful, pure, gentle, and friendly. I know a lot of people who are very intelligent, but they are also obnoxious. They know it all. They're not friendly. They're not peaceful. They're not gentle. They go around trying to impress everyone with their knowledge. If you're a truly wise person, you're gentle.

I once read a book called *Patton's Principles: For Managers Who Mean It.* It was filled with short statements by General

George Patton. One of the principles he stated is this: Never fight a battle when you won't gain anything by winning. Do you ever fight those kinds of battles in your marriage? Have you ever argued over a meaningless date?

"It was in 1982."

"No, it was 1983."

"No, it wasn't. It was 1982."

"No, it was. . . ."

Who cares? Never fight a battle in which you won't win anything. Your relationship with your spouse is worth more than the point you are trying to prove. Most of the time no one really cares when it happened anyway. Maybe you and your spouse have been at a dinner party, and your mate starts telling a story. You say, "Now honey, it wasn't that way. Remember, it was Aunt Mary, not Aunt Sue." Do you think the other people listening care which aunt it was? No. Not at all. Don't let your ego get involved. Be wise. Be gentle.

Gentleness is the ability to *disagree agreeably*. You can walk hand in hand with someone without seeing eye to eye. Anyway, if two people agree on everything, one of them is not needed. Gentleness is the ability to disagree agreeably.

Writing to Timothy, Paul said, "The Lord's servant must not quarrel; instead, he must be kind to everyone, able to teach, not resentful. Those who oppose him he must gently instruct, in the hope that God will grant them repentance leading them to a knowledge of the truth" (2 Tim. 2:24-25). Paul is saying that gentleness is a qualification for spiritual leadership. Do you know what that says to me? It says that if I am a leader, I am not to get swept up into arguments. You and I are not to get involved in petty disagreements and pointless conflicts. Specifically, this verse says that pastors are to be gentle with any opposition to their leadership and gently instruct them.

So far we've discussed three aspects of gentleness: be understanding, not demanding; be gentle, not judgmental; and be tender, without surrender. You don't have to give up your convictions, but you do need to be tender in the way you express them. Let's look at a fourth aspect.

Be Teachable, Not Unreachable

When someone *corrects* you, *be teachable, not unreachable.* James 1:19 says, "Let every man be quick to listen but slow to use his tongue, and slow to lose his temper" (PH). If you do the first two things, the third one naturally falls into place. If you are quick to listen and slow to answer back, you're going to be slow to lose your temper. Proverbs 13:18 says, "Whoever heeds correction is honored." If you want to be a gentle person, use your ears more than your mouth, and be willing to accept correction.

Now let me ask you husbands, when your wife comes to you and makes a suggestion, do you get defensive? Do you take every comment as a personal threat to your manhood? The Greek word translated "gentle" is sometimes translated "meek." I don't like the word *meekness* because meekness, unfortunately, rhymes with weakness. People tend to equate meekness with weakness. It's like the wife who said to her husband, "Are you a man or a mouse? Now squeak up!"

But Jesus said, "'Blessed are the meek." The Greek word translated here as "meek" also means "gentle." "Blessed are the meek, for they will inherit the earth" (Matt. 5:5). What do you think of when I say the word *meek?* Probably a doormat. Maybe you imagine a picture of Caspar Milquetoast, Pee Wee Herman, or a little kitten cowering in a corner. And yet, Jesus called Himself "meek" (Matt. 11:29, KJV), and He certainly wasn't afraid of anyone. The meek, the gentle, will inherit the earth because they are God's kind of people; they are like Jesus Christ.

The wisest people I know are the people most willing to

learn from others. They are always learning. I admire that in people. I admire people who have an attitude of "teach me." I've discovered that I can learn from anyone. You can too. You can learn from anyone if you just know the right questions to ask. It's important that you never stop asking questions because the moment you are through learning in life, you're through! Be teachable, not unreachable.

Let me ask you, from whom are you willing to learn? Can you learn from your husband? Or does that threaten you? Can you learn from your wife? Or does that threaten you? Can you learn from your kids? I've learned so much from my kids.

Let me tell you how to end up lonely in life: never admit any mistakes. Never learn from anyone. Never let anyone teach you anything. I guarantee you'll end up being a very lonely person. Nobody has all the answers. I don't. You don't. No one does. So we must all keep on learning. It's like the man who was a witness in court and the bailiff said, "Do you swear to tell the truth, the whole truth and nothing but the truth, so help you God?" The man answered, "Sir, if I knew the whole truth and nothing but the truth, I would be God!" That's true. None of us have all the answers. Gentleness involves being willing to learn from others.

Gentleness is also being willing to admit when you are wrong. How long has it been since you admitted to your spouse, "Honey, I was wrong. It was my fault"? Some people haven't said that in years.

James 1:21 says this is also the attitude we should have when we come to God's Word: "Humbly accept the word planted in you." Notice that word *humbly*. In Greek the word *humble* and the word *gentle* are the same word. It's the same word as meekness. It means to be teachable, not unreachable. When we approach God's Word, we ought to approach it with a gentle or humble attitude, saying, "God, I'm willing to be taught."

Be an Actor, Not a Reactor

When someone *hurts* you, *be an actor, not a reactor*. By "actor" I don't mean hypocrite or pretender, but one who *initiates* the action. Be an actor, not a reactor. The Apostle Peter recalled how Jesus acted at His trial before Pilate. "When they hurled their insults at Him, He did not retaliate; when He suffered, He made no threats. Instead, He entrusted Himself to Him who judges justly" (1 Peter 2:23). While Pilate was questioning Him, Jesus could have commanded all the angels in heaven to come down and rescue Him in an instant. The trial was not even legal. But Jesus endured the trial in silence. Let me ask you, who was really in control of that situation, Pilate or Jesus? The psychological dynamics of that confrontation are fascinating. Pilate was threatened by the simple fact that Jesus wouldn't speak up and defend Himself. It made Pilate nervous. Rather than react to Pilate, Jesus assumed control of the situation by choosing to remain silent. He didn't need to react to Pilate's insults because He knew exactly who He was, the Son of God.

When someone hurts you, be an actor, not a reactor. Strength is found in gentleness. And gentleness is the ability to handle hurt without retaliating. It's the ability to absorb the blow without striking back. Jesus called it "turning the other cheek." You say, "That's not easy to do." No, it's not; it's almost impossible. "To respond that way is not natural," you say. You're right. It's supernatural; it's the fruit of the Spirit. You need God's power to live this way.

When someone at work stabs you in the back, what do you do? Do you pull out your big guns and react? Maybe you say, "You make me so mad!" When you say that, you are admitting that someone else is controlling your emotions. You are acknowledging that you've given that person the power to determine your feelings and reactions. Remember this: no one can *take* that control from you. You give it away the moment you start reacting. If someone is unfaithful to you, do you react by being unfaithful to that person? Learn to be an actor, not a reactor.

God's Word tells us: "Do not repay evil for evil. . . . Do not be overcome by evil, but overcome evil with good" (Rom. 12:17-21). That's the power of action rather than reaction. To retaliate is to react. To forgive is to act. It's saying, "I choose the way I respond."

Sydney Harris, a syndicated columnist, tells of accompanying a friend to a newsstand and watching his friend greet the salesman very courteously. In return, however, he received gruff, discourteous service, as the salesman rudely shoved the newspaper in his direction. Harris' friend politely smiled and wished the man a nice weekend. As they walked on down the street, Sydney Harris asked his friend, "Does he always treat you so rudely?"

"Yes, unfortunately, he does."

"Are you always so polite and friendly to him?"

"Yes, I am."

"Why are you so nice to him when he's so unfriendly to you?"

Get this line—it's a classic: "Because I don't want him to decide how I'm going to react." That's gentleness. That's strength under control. Choosing the way I respond to people. That's choosing to be an actor rather than a reactor.

Do you let other people control your emotional state? Do you let people either raise your happiness level or plunge you into worry, fear, or anger? Proverbs 16:32 says, "He who is slow to anger is better than the mighty, and he who rules his spirit than he who takes a city" (NKJV). This verse is saying that the person who can control his moods is stronger than an army in a city that has a wall around it. But a person who can't control his own spirit is defenseless, like a city with no walls around it. You have no defense, because you're at the mercy of whatever anyone wants to do to you. We'll say more about this in the next chapter when we look at the fruit of self-control.

Be Respectful
There's one last type of person with whom you should practice gentleness—unbelievers. When you witness to people, when you share your faith, *respect them, don't reject them.* Have you noticed that a lot of evangelism is just a thinly veiled put-down? We share the Gospel with a sense of superiority: "You need what I've got because you are so bad." The fact is people do need the Good News, but our attitude can keep them from receiving it. Respect unbelievers, don't put them down. Respecting them means you accept them. That doesn't mean that you must approve of their lifestyle. There's a difference between acceptance and approval. I can accept you as a person of worth without approving of everything you do. And I must respect your right to be treated in a respectful way.

First Peter 3:15 says, "Always be prepared to give an answer to everyone who asks you to give the reason for the hope that you have. But do this with *gentleness* and *respect*" (emphasis added). The manner in which you share the Gospel can determine how willing a person is to listen to you. In fact, your attitude speaks more powerfully than the words of your message. Some people, unfortunately, use the Gospel as a sledgehammer.

There are two ways to get an egg out of an eggshell. One way is to crack it open; the other way is to put it in a warm, loving environment and let it incubate and hatch itself. The second way preserves the baby chick, while the first way kills it. Likewise, there are two ways to get the Good News across to people. You can pound them over the head with it, or you can love them into the family of God. The most effective way to share the Gospel with unbelievers is to surround them with love and acceptance as you share the Gospel with them. Be gentle. Respect them, don't reject them. D.T. Niles said, "Evangelism is just one beggar telling another where to find bread."

Jesus was gentle, and He wants us to be gentle in telling others about Him. Gentleness was natural to Jesus, but it doesn't come naturally to most of us. We must learn to be gentle.

One of the positive benefits of becoming more gentle is a more relaxed lifestyle. You will become more adaptable, more able to roll with the punches. One reason so many people experience emotional burnout is that they are not gentle. They're always demanding their rights. They judge others. They always have to prove their point. They are unwilling to learn from others. They react to situations, usually in anger or fear. And they seldom treat others with respect or dignity.

Now do you see just how important gentleness is for a healthy and happy life? Take stock of your life for a few minutes. In which relationships do you find it difficult to be gentle? Be specific. Write down your problem areas and put the list in your Bible. Then as you're reading the Word and praying, talk to God about those relationships and ask Him to help you be gentle with those people. Remember, you can't do it by yourself, no matter how much willpower you have. Gentleness is a fruit of the Spirit. A805

Chapter Eleven

DEVELOPING
SELF-CONTROL

So many of your problems and mine are caused by a lack of self-control. Why can't I lose weight? Why can't I hold onto a job? Why can't I keep the house clean? Why can't I get more done? Why can't I break that bad habit? Why can't I get in shape? Why can't I get out of debt? I can't do these things because I need self-control. My biggest problem is me!

Perhaps, like many people today, you feel your life is out of control—and maybe it is. You feel overwhelmed by circumstances and pressures. You feel defenseless and vulnerable. Like a car with a broken steering wheel, you screech around curves with no sense of control over the steering. That's a scary feeling. Proverbs 25:28 says, "Like a city whose walls are broken down is a man who lacks self-control."

Self-control brings with it the good feeling of competency. Like a finely tuned precision automobile, your life stays on course with the slightest touch of steering. The results of self-control are confidence and an inner sense of security.

Self-control and self-discipline are also key factors in any success you hope to have in this life. Without self-discipline you are unlikely to achieve anything of lasting value. The Apostle Paul realized this when he wrote, "Every athlete in training submits to strict discipline, in order to be crowned with a wreath that will not last; but we do it for one that will last forever" (1 Cor. 9:25, GNB). "No pain, no gain," is the way the fitness trainers put it, and they're right. Peak performance requires self-discipline and self-control. Olympic athletes train for years in order to have a chance to win a brief moment of glory. But the race we are running is·far more important than any earthly athletic event. So self-control is not optional for Christians.

If we are to achieve true freedom, we need self-control. The Greek philosopher Epictetus was right when he said, "No man is truly free until he masters himself." Jesus expressed it in these words: "Everyone who sins is a slave to sin" (John 8:34). Samson may have been the strongest man in the world, but he was enslaved by his lusts and desires because he lacked self-control. Strength without self-control got him into trouble.

People will try almost anything to gain self-control, or to make up for the lack of it. Have you noticed that? Pills, therapy, seminars, resolutions, surgery—people try them all. One advertisement for a weight-loss program has this heading: "If you've never succeeded at losing weight permanently, maybe you need a little inside help." I thought, *Great. That's right up my alley. The Bible says to be strong in the inner man—inner control.* So I read on: "You're fed up with weight loss programs, right? You've tried nearly every one, only to put the weight right back on. Well, there's something you should know. Overeating is not just a bad habit. It's a disease. And like any other, you can't treat it on your own. You need professional help. You can get it from (Are you ready for this?) the *Gastric Bubble Program.* . . . Here's how it works. A plastic bubble is inserted into your stomach, without surgery. Two things happen. It takes up a large space, causing you to eat less. And it decreases your appetite. *The result: You lose weight." (Orange County Register,* April 18, 1985). As I said, people will try almost anything to gain more self-control—or to make up for their lack of it.

Well, if these "quick and easy" answers don't bring self-control, how do we get it? How do we gain real self-control? God's Word is quite clear on this subject. Let me suggest seven steps to self-control.

Admit Your Problem

The first step in developing self-control is to accept responsibility for your lack of self-control. Admit your problem. James 1:14 says, "A man's temptation is due to the pull of *his own inward desires,* which greatly attract him" (PH, emphasis added). Do you realize what that says? It says you do things because you *like* to! When I do something I know is bad for me, I still do it because I like to do it. I want to do it. It's an inner desire.

We often try to ignore our problems or deny we have them: "I don't have a problem. What problem?" We often rationalize: "It's just the way I am." Or "Everybody else is doing it." Sometimes we blame others: "If I just had different parents." Or "The devil made me do it." You know, we can blame anyone, but as long as we waste our energy fixing the blame, we cannot fix the problem.

James says we like to take the course of least resistance, and giving in to temptation is usually that easiest course. The starting point for developing self-control is to face what God has already said about me: I am responsible for my behavior. Do you want more self-control? The first step is to admit that you have a problem and be specific about it. "I have this problem. This is where I need help." You may have a problem with food, drink, words, your temper, money, exercise, sex, clothes, time—all these different areas need self-control. Begin praying specifically about your problem areas.

Put Your Past behind You

The second step in developing self-control, and this is very important, is to put your past behind you. Notice what Paul says in Philippians 3:13-14, "Forgetting what is behind and straining toward what is ahead, I press on toward the goal." This verse exposes a misconception that will keep you from gaining self-control: once a failure, always a failure. You may say, "Oh, I tried to quit my bad habit. In fact, I've tried 15 times. I guess I will never be able to get control of this." That's a misconception. Failure in the past does not mean you'll never be able to change. Focusing on past failures, however, does guarantee their repetition. It's like driving a car and looking in the rearview mirror the whole time. You're going to collide with what's ahead of you. You've got to put your past behind you.

Have you watched a baby just learning to walk? He may fall down a lot, but he doesn't stay down. He keeps on trying, and ultimately he succeeds. A baby learns to walk by persistence. Can you imagine where you would be if you had given up when you tripped and fell two or three times? *It's hopeless. I'm a failure. I'll never be a walker. Let's just face it. Some people are meant to be walkers, and some people are not meant to be walkers. I just know I'm not meant to be a walker because I have tried and failed three times.*

The first time I kissed a girl, I was very nervous. I mean, I didn't want us to bump noses. So I sort of turned my head a little bit, and she turned her head a little bit, and we aimed for a connection. I'm embarrassed to admit what happened next. She had long hair and my glasses got caught in her hair. My first kiss was a fiasco. But I'm so glad I didn't give up on kissing!

Put your past behind you. It doesn't matter how many times you've failed. Try again. Only this time try a new way, admitting you have a problem. Put the past behind you. As Thomas Edison once said, "Don't call it a failure, call it an education! Now you know what doesn't work!"

Talk Back to Your Feelings

The next step in becoming more self-controlled is to talk back to your feelings. Challenge them. We put far too much emphasis on our feelings today. We think everything has to feel good or it's not worthwhile. "I don't feel like studying. I don't feel like working. I don't feel like getting out of bed. I don't feel like reading my Bible. I don't feel like washing the car." Or, "I feel like another helping of food or another drink. I feel like watching TV for 10 hours." Don't give your feelings so much authority. Feelings are highly unreliable.

Let me ask you, do you let your moods manipulate you? God doesn't want you to be controlled by your feelings. He wants you to master your moods. With Christ as the Master of your life you *can* learn to master your feelings. Talk back to them. God says He wants you to learn how to challenge your emotions.

For instance, let's say you're fighting the battle of the bulging waistline. Before you ever walk into the kitchen and open the refrigerator door you have begun to talk to yourself about eating. If you're serious about losing weight, you'll have to challenge some of those subconscious attitudes about food. When you hear yourself saying to yourself, "I've just *got* to take a snack or I'll die," you'll have to talk back to yourself and say something like, "No, I'm not going to die if I don't eat a snack. In fact, I'll be healthier if I don't."

In Titus 2:11-12 we read: "For the grace of God . . . teaches us to say no to ungodliness and worldly passions, and to live self-controlled, upright and godly lives." God's grace gives us the power to do what is right. God gives you the ability to say no to that feeling, to that desire, to that impulse. It's a supernatural power. With God's help you can master your moods.

Believe You Can Change

If you are going to change and become more self-controlled, you have to start believing you can change. The truth is that your beliefs do control your behavior. In almost every chapter I've mentioned that the fruit of the Spirit begins in your thought life. The seed must be planted in your mind. The way you think determines the way you feel, and the way you feel determines the way you act.

The person who says, "I can't do it," and the person who says, "I can do it," are both right. Much of the time you set yourself up to be defeated by a habit by saying, "I could never stop this. It's just the way I am. I'll never be able to change." Your own belief becomes a self-fulfilling prophecy.

Three times in 1 Peter, God reminds us to be clear-minded and self-controlled. Why? Because a clear mind has a lot to do with self-control. God gave us the power to change our habits when He gave us the power to choose our thoughts. Does Romans 12:2 tell us to be transformed by working hard at it or by sheer willpower? No. What are we to be transformed by? The renewing of the mind. When your self-control is being tested, you need to fill your mind with the promises of God. Let's look at one of God's beautiful promises.

First Corinthians 10:13 says, "God is faithful; He will not let you be tempted beyond what you can bear. But when you are tempted, He will also provide a way out so that you can stand up under it." That's a fact. If you are a Christian you cannot ever say, "The temptation was too strong; I couldn't help myself." The Bible says God is faithful. If you're a Christian, He won't let you be tempted beyond what you can bear. He never puts more *on* you than He puts *in* you to bear it.

So focus on God's positive promises of help and strength. Philippians 4:13 says, "I can do all things through Christ who strengthens me" (NKJV). I *can* change. I can be different. Stop setting yourself up for failure by constantly criticizing yourself. Stop nagging, condemning, and putting yourself down: "Oh, I'm worthless. I'm no good. I shouldn't even go to church. I simply have no control over my life." Nagging doesn't work— on yourself or anyone else! Instead, remember that Jesus says "Everything is possible for him who believes" (Mark 9:23).

Make Yourself Accountable

The fifth step in developing your self-control is a tough one: make yourself accountable to someone. We don't like this step, but we desperately need it. Find someone who will check up on you, who will pray for you, and who will encourage you in the area where you want to develop more self-control. Ecclesiastes 4:12 says, "Two men can resist an attack that would defeat one man alone" (GNB). That's the value of the Alcoholics Anonymous' approach, the "buddy" system, where you are encouraged to call someone whenever you feel the pressure building to return to old, destructive ways. Galatians 6:2 says, "Share each other's troubles and problems, and so obey our Lord's command" (TLB).

Let me suggest a project. If you are serious about self-control, find someone in your church and go to him or her and say, "I have this problem. I've confessed it to God. I've asked forgiveness, and now I want to ask you to help me. Will you be my 'buddy,' a person I can call on the phone when I need support and encouragement?" I believe God intends for every church to be filled with "buddy" relationships where people are accountable to each other, relationships where people help and encourage each other in the Lord. Having someone hold you accountable is tough, but it works.

What should you look for in a "buddy"? Several things. First, men should have a man "buddy" and women a woman. When two people share their struggles, a natural bond of closeness develops and leads to intimacy. You don't need to place another temptation in your path by sharing personal problems with someone of the opposite sex. Second, you should look for someone you can depend on to follow through on this commitment, someone who is faithful. And look for someone who will keep your problem confidential. Don't choose someone who is known to talk too much. One final thing that will help make this "buddy" system work: tell your "buddy" he or she has your permission to check up on you from time to time. Give him or her the right to ask you, "How are you doing with your problem?" Knowing that someone will be asking you about your problem is an additional incentive not to give in to temptation. That may be the extra push you need to get you moving on the road to victorious self-control.

Avoid Temptation

The sixth step to becoming more self-controlled is just common sense: avoid the things that tempt you. Stay away from situations that weaken your self-control. If you don't want to be stung, stay away from the bees.

As a youth director, I used to tell kids, "At this stage in your life your sexual drive is so powerful you must prepare in advance to control it. When you go on a date, you'll either be guided by your plans or by your glands! So plan what you will do and won't do on the date. The time to begin to think about exercising self-control is not in the backseat of a car."

Plan in advance to avoid situations that you know are going to cause temptation in your life. Don't keep candy in the cupboard if you are trying to diet. Don't acquire credit cards if you are an impulsive spender. Plan your life to avoid the things that weaken your self-control.

Ephesians 4:27 says, "Don't give the devil a chance" (GNB). Don't give him a foothold in your life. I once talked to one man who had quit smoking, and I asked him how he succeeded. He said, "I wet my matches!" In the time it took him to try to light a cigarette, he was back in control.

What in your life do you need to avoid? What do you need to get rid of? Maybe some magazines? Maybe some books or videos in your home? Maybe you need to break off a relationship you know is bad for you. First Corinthians 15:33 says, "Bad company corrupts good character." You may need to stay away from some people. Maybe every time you are around certain people you give in to temptation. The Bible warns us about friends like that. Avoid the people and situations that tempt you to forfeit self-control.

There's a wonderful children's book entitled *Frog and Toad Together* by Arnold Lobel. This is from a section called "Cookies":

Toad baked some cookies. "These cookies smell very good," said Toad. He ate one. "And they taste even better," he said. Toad ran to Frog's house. "Frog, Frog," cried Toad, "taste these cookies that I have made."

Frog ate one of the cookies. "These are the best cookies I have ever eaten!" said Frog. Frog and Toad ate many cookies, one after another. "You know, Toad," said Frog with his mouth full, "I think we should stop eating. We will soon be sick."

"You are right," said Toad. "Let's eat one last cookie, and then we will stop." Frog and Toad ate one last cookie. There were many cookies left in the bowl. "Frog," said Toad, "let's eat one very last cookie and then we will stop." Frog and Toad ate one very last cookie. "We must stop eating," cried Toad as he ate another.

"Yes," said Frog, reaching for a cookie, "we need will power."

"What is will power?" asked Toad.

"Will power is trying hard *not* to do something that you really want to do."

"You mean like trying *not* to eat all of these cookies?" asked Toad.

"Right," said Frog. Frog put the cookies in a box. "There," he said. "Now we won't eat any more cookies."

"*But* we can open the box," said Toad.

"That is true," said Frog. Frog tied some string around the box. "There," he said. "Now we will not eat any more cookies."

"*But* we can cut the string and open the box," said Toad.

"That is true," said Frog. Frog got a ladder. He put the box up on a high shelf. "There," said Frog. "Now we will not eat any more cookies."

"*But* we can climb the ladder and take the box down from the shelf and cut the string and open the box," said Toad.

"That is true," said Frog. Frog climbed the ladder and took the box down from the shelf. He cut the string and opened the box. Frog took the box outside. He shouted in a large, loud voice, "HEY, BIRDS. HERE ARE COOKIES." Birds came from everywhere. They picked up all the cookies in their beaks and flew away.

"Now we have no more cookies to eat," said Toad sadly. "Not even one."

"Yes," said Frog, "but we have lots and lots of will power!"

"You may keep it all, Frog," said Toad. "I'm going home to bake a cake" (Harper & Row. Used by permission.)

That's about as strong as some of our willpower is! The point is this: What in your life do you need to feed to the birds? What do you need to avoid? You may need to change your job because a relationship there is wrong and is harming you. That's a drastic measure, but you may need to do something that significant in order to avoid whatever is tempting you at this particular time. You know you are not strong enough to resist it right now.

Let's review the steps for developing self-control that we've discussed so far: admit your problem; put the past behind you; talk back to your feelings; start believing you can change; make yourself accountable to someone; avoid the things that tempt you. Now there's one more step, and it's the secret of lasting self-control.

Depend on Christ's Power

If you want to develop self-control, learn to depend on Christ's power to help you. Galatians 5:16 says, "Let the Spirit direct your lives, and you will not satisfy the desires of the human nature" (GNB). Notice the sequence in this sentence. It's very important. Let the Spirit direct your life—that's the first part—and you will not satisfy the desires of the human nature. Notice, it does not say you won't *have* those desires. Spirit-filled people are still going to have the desires of the flesh. It just says you won't satisfy them.

We usually get the sequence backward. What we usually say is, "I'm not good enough to have God's Spirit in my life. I'm not worthy to have Him direct me. My life is a mess. Once I get my act together, once I've got this habit under control, then I'm going to come to God and really live for Him. Then I'm going to let the Holy Spirit control my life . . . after I've got it all together." God says, "No, that's not the sequence." He doesn't say, "Get your act together and *then* I will help you." Rather, God says, "Let Me into your life. Let My Holy Spirit control you *while* you're still struggling with that problem. I will help you change." The sequence makes an incredible difference.

What would you think if I said, "I'm going to get well first, and then I'm going to go see the doctor." You'd say I was crazy. It's a ridiculous idea. "I'm going to feel better; then I'll take the medicine." It's absurd, but I hear people say things like that all the time. "You know, Rick, I'm going to break this bad habit and then start attending church. I'm going to clean up my life, and then I'll commit it to Christ." Or, "I've got a problem in my life, and I'm going to wait until that problem is resolved, and then I'm going to be baptized." The truth is you need Christ in your life *now* to help you get over the problem. He has the power to help you change.

I've also heard many people say, "I'm not good enough to be a Christian, so I'm not even going to try." Fine! Don't try, just trust. Put your trust in Christ and depend on Him to change what you've been unable to change. And find a church where you can grow. The church is a hospital for sinners, not a hotel for saints. The church is for people who are hurting. The church is for people who don't have it all together but are honest enough to say, "We're not perfect, but we want to grow. And we're all in this together."

Perhaps you say, "I know where I lack self-control, and I know what I'm doing is wrong, but I still like doing it." So what? Do you think that surprises God? The Bible says there is pleasure in sin for a season. What does that mean? It means sin is fun—at least for a while. None of us would sin if sin immediately made us miserable.

Notice what Philippians 2:13 says: "For God is at work within you, helping you to want to obey Him, and then helping you to do what He wants" (TLB). Isn't that a great verse? It says that God not only gives you the desire to do right, but He also gives you the power to do what is right. But you must have Him in your life first.

In what area(s) of your life do you have a hard time saying no? Do you have a hard time saying no to food? Do you have a hard time saying no to excessive spending? Alcohol? Drugs? Illicit sex? Cigarettes? Do you have trouble saying no to your feelings? Maybe you are really struggling with an addiction. Maybe nobody else knows about it, but the Lord knows about it. And He cares about you. But the best part is that He is able to do something about it. Will you stop right now and prayerfully think through these seven steps, asking God to help you start down the road to self-control?

The secret of self-control is Christ's control. If you still haven't done so, ask Him to take control of your life right now. Then, as you face temptations that are too strong for you to resist, remember that He is with you and turn them over to Him. Remember, Christ provides the power to change your life!

Chapter Twelve

A
PRODUCTIVE LIFE

Have you ever wondered why some people are able to accomplish so much with their lives? What makes them so productive? In America, we're very conscious of productivity at all levels. Once a month the government releases a report on our Gross National Product. It tells us how productive our businesses and industries have been. It's an important picture of our national economic health.

Suppose each of us were issued an individual Productivity Report each month. How would yours look? Would it show positive or negative results? Growth or decline? Think about the future. What do you want to do so at the end of your life you'll be able to say, "I led a productive life. I accomplished what I set out to accomplish"? Have you ever defined what you consider to be a productive life? More important, do you know God's definition of a productive, fruitful life? What does it mean to be a fruitful Christian?

The word *fruit* is used 66 times in the New Testament. Three different kinds of fruit are mentioned. The first kind is natural fruit: figs, grapes, raisins. This is the kind of fruit you eat. The Bible also mentions biological fruit: babies. The third kind of fruit is spiritual fruit: Christlike character. In the preceding chapters, we've looked at the fruit of the Spirit: love, joy, peace, patience, kindness, goodness, faithfulness, gentleness, and self-control. God wants to see that kind of fruit in our lives. That is His definition of a productive life.

In John 15:8, Jesus says, "This is to my Father's glory, that you bear much fruit, showing yourselves to be My disciples."

The proof that you are a disciple is that you bear fruit. "You did not choose me," Jesus goes on to say, "but I chose you and appointed you to go and bear fruit—fruit that will last" (John 15:16). God wants us to bear fruit, much fruit. He wants us to be productive. In this final chapter we'll look at the four conditions for fruitfulness that are given in the Bible.

Cultivate Roots

If I want to be fruitful, I must *cultivate some roots*. God says that without roots there will be no fruit. Jeremiah 17:7-8 says, "Blessed is the man who trusts in the Lord, whose confidence is in Him. He will be like a tree planted by water that sends out its roots by the stream. It does not fear when the heat comes; its leaves are always green. It has no worries in a year of drought and never fails to bear fruit." You must have good roots in order to bear fruit. If you don't have any roots, you simply won't bear any fruit.

Now, why do we need roots? This passage gives one reason: We need roots to make it through tough times—times of heat and times of drought. Roots are the lifeline of nourishment for the entire plant or tree. Have you ever felt the heat in life, times when the pressure is on? I'm sure you can recall those stressful times. That's when you needed roots.

I grew up near the giant redwoods in northern California. Amazingly, redwood trees can withstand major forest fires. And they can even survive with four- or five-foot gashes in their trunks because of their tremendous roots. Or take a more common tree like the oak. The roots of a large oak tree, if you were to place them end to end, would stretch out several hundred miles. That's why oak trees are so stable.

I read some time ago about the banana tree. It's almost indestructible. You can chop it into little pieces, but it will grow back. You can burn it down, but it will grow back. There's only one way to get rid of a banana tree, and that's by uprooting it. The roots are the key to the fruit.

Proverbs 12:3 says that "the righteous cannot be uprooted." The righteous man can stand the heat. He can also endure a time of drought, a long season without rain. In a drought, resources are limited. Everything dries up, and many things die. But the righteous endure. Have you learned that sometimes in life you have to do without things on which you normally depend?

You may be going through a drought right now. Maybe you're doing without emotional support. You're doing without friends, or health, or a job, or financial stability. Or you're trying to get by on limited time, energy, or money. You're in a drought. How do you handle the dry spells in life? Do you wilt? Do you dry up and blow away?

If you ever visit the Arizona desert, you'll find it is full of different kinds of vegetation. The contrasts have always fascinated me. The dried up, brittle tumbleweed blows everywhere. Why? Because it has no roots. By contrast, the saguaro cactus bears fruit even in 130 degree weather. Why? Because the saguaro cactus has roots that go out 50 to 60 feet in all directions. You've got to have roots if you are going to make it through a dry spell.

Anyone can survive a day of drought, but surviving an extended time of stress is another matter. For instance, if the cash flow in your business is bad for a month, you'll probably say, "Well, we'll make it up next month." But by the end of the second month, if things don't pick up, you'll begin to get a little anxious. By the third month you'll start to panic, and by the fourth month you'll probably fight major depression—unless you have some roots.

How do you cultivate roots? A good place to begin is memorizing Psalm 1:2-3. The psalmist talks about the stable life, the life that has roots. He says roots are developed by reading and meditating on God's Word. We learn the same thing in the

New Testament, in Colossians 2:6-7. Spend time daily reading, meditating on, memorizing, and obeying God's Word. That's how you develop strong spiritual roots, roots that go deep into the soil of God's Word. These roots will enable you to withstand the heat of pressure and the deprivation of drought.

Eliminate Weeds

The second thing you need to do in order to be productive is to *eliminate the weeds* in your life. Jesus illustrates this in the Parable of the Soils. He mentions four kinds of soil. Each type of soil represents one of the ways we can respond to God's Word. In Luke 8:11-14, we read: "The seed is the Word of God . . . and the seed that falls among [weeds] stands for those who hear the Word, but the worries, riches, and pleasures of this life crowd in and choke their lives and their fruit never ripens" (GNB). If you want to bear fruit, you've got to cultivate good roots and then eliminate the weeds.

Here's a trivia question for you: How many kinds of weeds grow in the United States? The government reports 205 varieties of weeds in the United States. I estimate that 72 percent of those are in my backyard. In fact, I've thought about opening an exhibition and charging admission: "Warren's Weed Farm." They're incredible.

What are the weeds in your life? Many different types of weeds can crowd into your life and choke the spiritual vitality out of you. Weeds are the concerns and interests that sap your time, energy, and money and prevent you from bearing spiritual fruit.

I have people tell me, "I just don't have time to serve the Lord. I'm too busy. I don't have time to get involved." If that's true in your life, then you're too busy! You need to do some weeding. Many things in life aren't necessarily wrong; they just aren't necessary. Maybe you need to cut back your schedule a bit. The person who burns the candle at both ends isn't as bright as he thinks he is. You can have so many irons in the fire that you put out the fire. You've got to eliminate the weeds.

Jesus mentions three varieties of weeds. First, there are the weeds of worry—the everyday cares and concerns that demand your attention. Then there are weeds of riches. Does your job dominate your life so much that you don't have any time for the Lord? Then it's a weed. The third kind of weed is pleasure. Yes, even pleasurable activities can become weeds. Chasing "the good life" can choke out your spiritual growth. Do you know people who put recreation first in their lives? It's fine to have a good time, but you need to guard your priorities. When the beach becomes more important than the Bible, your priorities are out of balance.

Now consider this: How much effort does it take to grow weeds? What do you have to do to cultivate them? Nothing! They grow very well on their own. That's why they're weeds. You have to nurse your tomato plants, but you don't have to do anything to grow dandelions. They will grow, and grow rapidly, with no help from you or anyone else.

Weeds are a sign of neglect, and when I neglect Bible reading, prayer, and fellowship with other Christians, weeds are going to grow up and choke my spiritual life. They will prevent me from bearing fruit. So if I'm going to bear fruit, I've got to deepen and cultivate my roots, and I've got to eliminate the weeds in my life.

Cooperate with God

If I'm going to be a fruitful Christian, I must *cooperate with God's pruning* in my life. In John 15:1-2, Jesus says, "I am the true vine, and my Father is the gardener. He lops off every branch that doesn't produce. And He prunes those branches that bear fruit for even larger crops" (TLB). Pruning involves *cutting off* the dead branches and *cutting back* the living branches, both to shape the tree or vine and to stimulate growth.

I have a neighbor named Ezra. He's an elderly Jewish man and a great guy. Ezra is an incredible rose grower. His front and back yards are just beautiful, so I invited him to come over to my backyard and work his magic on my roses. He was a wonder to watch. He brought his loppers over to do his pruning, and he was ruthless. It hurt me just to watch him cut back my rose bushes. Whack, whack, whack! By the time he was finished, my rose bushes were only little stubs. Professional pruners will tell you that most people are too timid when it comes to pruning. I used to think that pruning was going in and gently cutting off the little dead pieces. Not so. The live stuff needs to go too—branches, leaves, and flowers. Evidently Ezra knew what he was doing because my roses have never bloomed so beautifully.

Now here's the point. Most of us think that when God prunes us, He cuts off the sinful and the superficial, the deadwood in our lives. He does do that, but He also cuts off stuff that is alive and successful: a business that's going great, a satisfying relationship, good health. Some of that may get whacked off for greater fruitfulness. It's not just deadwood that goes. God often cuts back good things too, in order to make you healthier. It's not always pleasant, but pruning is absolutely essential for spiritual growth. It is not optional. Remember, God is glorified when we bear "much fruit" (John 15:8), and that requires pruning. We must remember that the loppers are in the hands of our loving God. He knows what He is doing, and He wants what is best for us.

If you are a Christian, you are going to be pruned. Count on it. You may be going through pruning right now, and it may not all be deadwood. God cuts off branches we may feel are productive in order that more fruit may be produced. That can be confusing. We feel we are being fruitful and are puzzled, even frustrated by God's pruning. "Why are You doing this, God? I've given my business to You, but it's failing. I've committed my health to You, and I'm going to the hospital next week. I've been tithing faithfully, and yet I'm going bankrupt." It may be pruning—God's pruning.

I watched an educational TV program on houseplants awhile ago. The specialist suggested viewers talk to their plants to help them grow. He explained that soothing, stroking, and talking to your Creeping Charlie will build the plant's self-esteem. Imagine yourself saying, "You're a good plant. My, you're looking good today. You look marvelous." Now imagine yourself talking to a plant you are pruning. "This hurts me more than it hurts you." Whack! "You'll thank me for this later!" Whack! "It's for your own good!" I can imagine the plant talking back, "You have no heart. You don't love me. I've worked long and hard to produce those roses you just cut off."

Isn't that what we say to God when He prunes us? "Don't You love me? Don't You care? Don't You see what's going on?" And we think God is angry with us. No, He's not angry. One of the biggest mistakes Christians make is confusing pruning with punishment. Pruning is not punishment. Don't equate the two. God is not angry with you. He just sees that you are someone who can bear more fruit, someone who has potential for greatness, someone He wants to use in a significant way. He wants you to be as fruitful as you possibly can be, so He prunes you back, even lopping off some of the things He's been blessing in your life. You lost your job? Don't worry. God has a better idea. He sees what you do not see.

Now, how does God prune us? He uses problems, pressures, and people. Oh, does he use people! People will criticize and challenge you. They'll question and doubt you. They'll challenge your motives. God is using them to prune you. What am I saying? I'm saying what I've been saying throughout this book: God can use every situation in your life to help you grow if you'll just have the right attitude. He can use it all: the problems you bring on yourself; a major disappointment; a financial reversal; a sudden illness; a marriage that breaks up; a rebellious child; the death of a loved one. He will and He does use them all as part of the pruning process to make you even more fruitful.

Why does God do this to us? Look at Hebrews 12:11: "No discipline seems pleasant at the time, but painful." We can all agree with that. It's not pleasant when you are being disciplined. The writer of Hebrews continues: "Later on, however, it produces a *harvest of righteousness and peace* for those who have been trained by it" (emphasis added). God does this for our own benefit as well as for His glory.

Like discipline, pruning is unpleasant. Have you ever looked at a pruned tree? Or a pruned plant? They are ugly. A few years ago I had 12 eucalyptus trees in my front yard that were about 60 feet tall. So I had a man come out and top them. He "topped" them all right—he left no branches! I ended up with 12 "totem poles" standing in my front yard. Some of my neighbors joked that a UFO had dropped these giant toothpicks in my front yard. I think some of them thought I was starting some kind of Stonehenge cult in the front yard. Those trees were ugly to look at. But do you know what? After that pruning, they came back with greater fullness than ever before. Now my problem is raking up all the leaves!

Pruning is never fun, and it's not pretty, but it's for your future benefit. The purpose of pruning is positive. God is not mad at you. The Bible says that there is no condemnation for those who are in Christ Jesus (Rom. 8:1). God does not "punish" His true children. Your punishment was taken care of on the cross. Now God's pruning is for your very best, for greater fruitfulness in your life.

My wife went through a time of severe pruning several

years ago. She was ill, had a tough pregnancy, and was bedridden for months. It was a very tough time for our family. God cut back every activity in Kay's life. I mean everything—leading women's ministry, teaching Bible studies, everything she loved and looked forward to doing. Even at home everything was chopped off because she couldn't get out of bed. We talked about it a lot because it didn't make sense at the time. Our church was growing rapidly, and I needed Kay's help. But it was a valuable pruning time. Kay learned so much because when you're flat on your back, all you can do is look up. Her fruitfulness in the years since has been astounding. God has opened up new ministries and opportunities for her that we never imagined. The results of that pruning in her life are exciting, but it wasn't fun going through it.

Can God's pruning fail to produce? Sure it can if we don't cooperate. If we resist, rebel, complain, or become resentful, our character won't develop the way God intends it to.

We've now looked at nine specific character qualities God wants to develop in your life: love, joy, peace, patience, kindness, goodness, faithfulness, gentleness, and self-control. How does God produce these qualities in your life? As I've said before, He does it by allowing you to encounter situations and people full of exactly the opposite qualities. He teaches you love by putting you around unlovely people. He teaches you joy in the midst of sorrow. He teaches you peace by allowing irritations all around you. He teaches you patience by allowing things to frustrate you. God uses all of those things to make you more fruitful, but you must cooperate with Him. The way you express that cooperation is by praising God in every circumstance (1 Thes. 5:18).

Wait for the Harvest

If I want my life to be fruitful, I must cultivate good roots, eliminate the weeds, and cooperate with God's pruning by thanking and praising Him. I must also *wait for the harvest.* Growth takes time. It's not instantaneous. God takes two days to make mushrooms; He takes 60 years to make an oak tree. Do you want to be a mushroom or an oak tree? Growth takes time.

When you examine your spiritual growth you may wonder, *Why is it taking me so long to get better? I've been a Christian for two years, and I don't see much change. I'm still struggling with my many weaknesses. Why?* Because spiritual growth, like natural growth, takes time. The best fruit ripens slowly.

Notice what Jesus says in John 12:24. He was talking about His death, but the principle here applies to us as well. He said, "Truly, truly, I say to you, unless a grain of wheat falls into the earth and dies, it remains alone; but if it dies, it bears much fruit" (RSV). When Jesus says, "Truly, truly," He is saying, "Now get this! Tune in!" He's saying, "Listen and listen good. This is really important."

The point Jesus stresses here is that death precedes life. Just as a grain of wheat must die to produce fruit, so must we die to ourselves to produce spiritual growth. And dying to our own selfishness takes time. Our tendency is to dig up the seed periodically to check on its progress, instead of trusting God to do His work in our lives. Christ will produce fruit in our lives if we remain in Him. In the passage on the vine and the branches in John 15, the key word is the word *remain*. We must *remain* in Him. Remember that word. Remaining in Christ means keeping in contact with Him, depending on Him, living for Him, and trusting Him to do *His* work in our lives in *His* perfect timing. Never give up. It's always too soon to quit! Wait for God's promised harvest and, in the meantime, enjoy His presence in your life. God is pleased with you at every stage of your spiritual growth. He's not waiting until you are perfect to begin loving you. He will never love you any more than He already does.

As you look back over the chapters in this book, are you seeing any spiritual fruit in your life? Perhaps you have memorized the ninefold fruit listed in Galatians 5:22-23. If not, I'd encourage you to do so. Think about how these qualities could be seen in the life of Jesus, and count on Him to produce them in you by the working of His Holy Spirit. If you're not seeing as much fruit as you'd like, don't despair. Remember that growth takes time. I recommend that you commit yourself to focus on one specific fruit of the Spirit each month for the next year. Use that month to study it in detail. Chapter 3 of my book *Dynamic Bible Study Methods* (Victor Books) explains step by step how you can do a personal Bible study on a character quality.

The four activities outlined in this chapter are the practical steps you need to take if you are serious about a fruitful, productive Christian life. Begin cultivating deep roots by spending time in God's Word every day. Then eliminate the weeds in your life that eat up your time and energy and distract you from doing God's will. Next, cooperate with God in the pruning process by thanking and praising Him for what He is doing in your life. He is working to make you more fruitful than you ever thought possible. Finally, wait expectantly for the harvest of spiritual fruit in your life. If you've followed the first three steps, the harvest is inevitable!

In 1968 a scientist discovered a 600-year-old seed necklace in an Indian grave. He planted one of the seeds, and it sprouted and grew. Dormant for 600 years, the potential for life was still there. Maybe you've been a Christian for years, and have been spiritually dormant for most of that time. But now you'd like to be productive. You desire to be fruitful. Your reading this book is evidence of that. I have good news for you. It's not too late! You can begin right now! Bow your head in prayer and tell God you want to cooperate with His growth plan for you. He will provide the power to change your life!